Contracts for Independent Readers

Fantasy

Grades 4–6

Writers:
Dee Benson, Rusty Fischer, Michael Foster, Beth Gress, Terry Healy, Kimberly Minafo,
Lori Sammartino, Louise Stearns, David Webb

Editors:
Kim T. Griswell and Cayce Guiliano

Contributing Editors:
Deborah T. Kalwat and Scott Lyons

Art Coordinator:
Donna K. Teal

Artists:
Nick Greenwood, Sheila Krill, Mary Lester,
Kimberly Richard, Rebecca Saunders, Donna K. Teal

Cover Artist:
Nick Greenwood

www.themailbox.com

©2001 by THE EDUCATION CENTER, INC.
All rights reserved.
ISBN #1-56234-405-6

Manufactured in the United States

10 9 8 7 6 5 4 3 2 1

Table of Contents

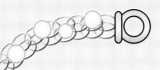
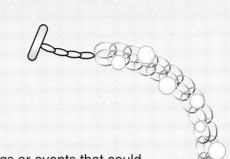

About This Book

What is fantasy?

Fantasy novels combine some elements of reality with beings or events that could not exist in real life. They include strange settings (other worlds or other times) and unusual characters (supernatural beings, tiny people, or animals that talk). They often deal with the issue of good versus evil. Fantasy helps develop children's imaginations and gives them a sense of escape from the burden of the real world.

How to use this book:

Contracts for Independent Readers—Fantasy includes everything you will need to implement an independent reading program in your classroom.

The **Teacher's Organizational Checklist** on page 4 will help you monitor your students' progress throughout the year. To use this page, photocopy it to make a class supply and write each student's name in the space provided. Hold a conference with each student to assess the goals the student has for the semester or the year. Have the student write her goals in the space provided. Next, have each student choose one of the novels included in this book to read. List the title of the book in the appropriate column. When the student has completed an activity, write the date it was completed in the bottom portion of the corresponding box. Use the key at the bottom of the page to note the type of activity completed in the top portion of the corresponding box as shown in the sample. After evaluating the activities, write any comments you have in the space provided and have the student do the same. At the end of the semester or year, direct each student to complete the self-assessment portion detailing how she feels she has done at reaching her goals. Finally, write your own assessment of each student's progress.

The **introductory page** of each independent contract contains a description of the novel, background information on the author, and a student contract materials list. This list will aid you in preparing in advance any materials that students may need. Most of the listed materials can be found right in the classroom!

Each of the two programmable **contract pages** in each unit has six independent activities for students to choose from. Each unit also includes **reproducible pages** that correspond to several independent activities. The second contract page has slightly more advanced activities than the first contract page.

Since some novels are at higher reading levels or may contain more mature content, we suggest that you read each of the novels so that you may assist students in choosing which novels to read.

Also included in this book is a **student booklist** on page 61, which consists of 12 fantasy novels, with a brief description of each. This list provides you with additional titles for students who finish early, for students who would enjoy reading other books in this genre, and for you to include in your classroom library.

> **Other Books in the Contracts for Independent Readers Series:**
> - *Contracts for Independent Readers—Historical Fiction*
> - *Contracts for Independent Readers—Humor*
> - *Contracts for Independent Readers—Realistic Fiction*
> - *Contracts for Independent Readers—Mystery*
> - *Contracts for Independent Readers—Adventure*

Name _____

Book Title

Sample: Book Title	Activity 1	Activity 2	Activity 3	Activity 4	Activity 5	Activity 6	Activity 7	Activity 8	Activity 9	Activity 10	Activity 11	Activity 12	Teacher Comments	Student Comments
	MA 11/6	SS 11/7			LA 11/10									

Student Goals:

Self-Assessment:

Teacher Assessment:

Key

LA = Language Arts
RD = Reading
W = Writing
MA = Math
SS = Social Studies
SC = Science
A = Art
MU = Music
RS = Research
CT = Critical Thinking

Ella Enchanted
by Gail Carson Levine

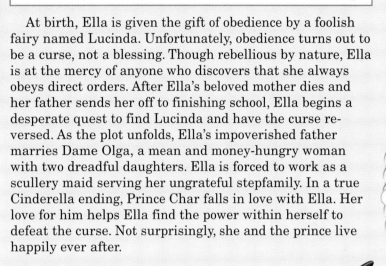

About the Book

At birth, Ella is given the gift of obedience by a foolish fairy named Lucinda. Unfortunately, obedience turns out to be a curse, not a blessing. Though rebellious by nature, Ella is at the mercy of anyone who discovers that she always obeys direct orders. After Ella's beloved mother dies and her father sends her off to finishing school, Ella begins a desperate quest to find Lucinda and have the curse reversed. As the plot unfolds, Ella's impoverished father marries Dame Olga, a mean and money-hungry woman with two dreadful daughters. Ella is forced to work as a scullery maid serving her ungrateful stepfamily. In a true Cinderella ending, Prince Char falls in love with Ella. Her love for him helps Ella find the power within herself to defeat the curse. Not surprisingly, she and the prince live happily ever after.

About the Author

Gail Carson Levine was born on September 17, 1947, in New York, New York. She grew up in the city and received her B.A. from City College in 1969. Today she lives in Brewster, New York, in a 200-year-old farmhouse with her husband, David Levine, and their Airedale, Jake.

Levine has been writing for most of her life. She had poems published in two student anthologies while she was in high school. She worked with her husband to write a children's musical called *Spacenapped,* which was produced by a small Brooklyn theater.

Levine has always loved fairy tales. She borrowed the plot for *Ella Enchanted* from *Cinderella.* By changing the original story's sweet, obedient character into the rebellious Ella, Levine has spun a wonderful story that has been described as fresh and charming. *Ella Enchanted* was recognized as a Newbery Honor Book in 1998. Levine has also written three other Princess Tales books: *The Fairy's Mistake, The Princess Test,* and *Princess Sonora and the Long Sleep.*

Student Contract Materials List

- Activity #1: copy of page 8
- Activity #2: drawing paper, crayons or markers, research materials on mythological creatures, stapler
- Activity #3: crayons or markers, research materials on fungi and mushrooms, white paper
- Activity #4: 12" x 18" construction paper or newsprint, colored pencils or markers
- Activity #5: 12" x 18" construction paper, crayons or markers

- Activity #6: graph paper or drawing paper, colored pencils or markers
- Activity #7: round balloon, plastic cup, star-shaped cutouts, tape, glue, arts-and-crafts supplies
- Activity #8: paper, pencil
- Activity #9: copy of page 9
- Activity #10: 8½" x 11" stationery, 10" length of narrow ribbon
- Activity #11: copy of page 10
- Activity #12: drawing paper, crayons or markers

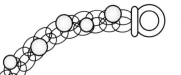

Ella Enchanted

Independent Contract

Name:_____ Number of activities to be completed: _____

1. Reading

Can a gift be a curse? It can if Lucinda is giving out the presents! Lucinda has only the best intentions, but she doesn't stop to consider the consequences of her gifts. Think about the gifts that Lucinda gives to Ella, the newlywed giants, and Sir Peter and Dame Olga. Consider some possible unexpected outcomes of each gift. Then obtain a copy of page 8 from your teacher and complete the activity as directed.

2. Language Arts

The creatures mentioned in *Ella Enchanted* are very different from those you are used to. Make a reference titled "Creature Features Picture Dictionary" to help strangers understand the physical characteristics and magical powers of unusual creatures. Feature illustrations and descriptions of ogres, dragons, giants, elves, gnomes, centaurs, gryphons, and at least seven other creatures mentioned in *Ella Enchanted*. Arrange the creature pages as they would be found in a dictionary or encyclopedia. Then staple the pages together along the left-hand side.

3. Science

In chapter 18, Mandy prepares the torlin kerru as ordered by Ella's father for the dinner with Edmund, Earl of Wolleck. Later we discover that fungi makes the earl ill. Are mushrooms in the fungus family? Research five mushrooms from the list below. Then create a five-page field guide to mushrooms. Tell where each mushroom can be found and whether it is edible, and give a detailed description of its physical characteristics. Add a title and decorate the cover of your booklet.

jack-o'-lantern	milk cap	honey
fairy-ring	bird's nest	earthstar
destroying angel	shaggy mane	

4. Social Studies

How do you picture Ella's enchanted world? Create a map of the kingdom where Ella lives. Include such places as the elves' Forest, the Fens, Frell, Jenn, King Jerrold's palace, and the royal menagerie. When the map is complete, create a well-used, antique look by wrinkling it and giving it tattered edges.

5. Writing

Although Ella is almost 15, her father, Sir Peter, hardly knows her. After her mother dies, Sir Peter says to Ella, "But who are you?" How would you respond if someone asked you the same question? Draw a large oval on a sheet of construction paper, leaving a border for a frame. Inside the oval, draw a self-portrait. Then, on the back, describe your physical characteristics and your personality traits. Give details about things you like and dislike, people who are important to you, and your goals. Decorate the frame with pictures of things that you treasure.

6. Math

Ella jokes with Char, first telling him she is too young to marry, then too old. How old do you think someone should be to get married? Survey at least 20 students to track popular opinions of the perfect age for marriage. Use a form of your own design to record the responses. Present the results in one of the following ways: a pictograph, a bar graph, or a pie graph. Be sure to include a title for your survey and a key for reading the graph.

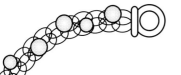

Ella Enchanted

Independent Contract

Name:_____ Number of activities to be completed: _____

7. Art

ZhulpH's grandmother predicts to Ella, "zhulpH is not the only one you will save. I see it." The gnome also sees danger, a quest, and three unfriendly people in Ella's future. Write each prediction on the front of a star shape. On the back, explain how the prediction comes true. Then decorate an inflated balloon to look like a crystal ball. Glue it to the top of a cup so it will stay in position. Tape the star predictions to the balloon to create a crystal ball revealing Ella's future.

8. Writing

The letters found throughout *Ella Enchanted* help the reader learn about the problems and feelings of various characters. Reread the letters from Dame Olga to her daughters in chapter 12 and from Hattie and Olive to their mother in chapter 16. Pretend you are Dame Olga. Write a letter to Olive describing your feelings about Ella's marriage, your husband being away, and how much you miss your daughter. Try to capture the personality and voice of Dame Olga in your writing.

9. Math

Imagine shopping in Ella's world, where they use brass, silver, and gold KJs instead of dollars. How many silver KJs would a dozen delicious quail eggs cost? How many dollars would that be equal to? Help Ella decide how much money she will need to complete her holiday shopping. Obtain a copy of page 9 from your teacher and complete the conversion chart as directed. When you are finished, the handy dollar-to-KJ conversion chart you made will give you all the information you need to help Ella buy gifts without going over her budget!

10. Music

Imagine that when Areida comes to the royal wedding of Ella and Char, she offers them the special gift of an Ayorthaian wedding song. Choose the music from a song that you know or create your own melody. Write lyrics to celebrate the joyous occasion in the traditional Ayorthaian style described in chapter 24. Write the lyrics on a fancy sheet of paper and present them in the form of a scroll tied with a ribbon. Perform your song for the class.

11. Critical Thinking

To hide her true identity from Prince Char, Ella appears at the three balls as Lela of Bast. Lela is an anagram of Ella. An anagram is a word or phrase scrambled into another word or phrase using the same letters. Anagrams are fun and challenging to solve. Obtain a copy of page 10 from your teacher and reveal the anagrams of familiar words.

12. Language Arts

When Ella and Char travel, they don't always take their children along. Ella's magic book keeps her connected to the children. How do the children stay connected to their parents? Create a five-page magic book for the royal children. Include a letter from Ella describing a new pet for the royal menagerie, a journal entry by Prince Char, and a fairy tale from both parents to their children. Add two other magical pages that young children might enjoy. Use fancy writing and decorate the pages with colorful illustrations. Don't forget to add an elegant cover!

No, Thanks!

That silly fairy Lucinda just won't learn her lesson! She keeps cursing people with her well-meant, though misguided, gifts.

Directions: Look at the presents shown below. Each present has a description of one of Lucinda's recent gifts. Carefully consider each gift and, on the back of this sheet, describe its possible negative consequences.

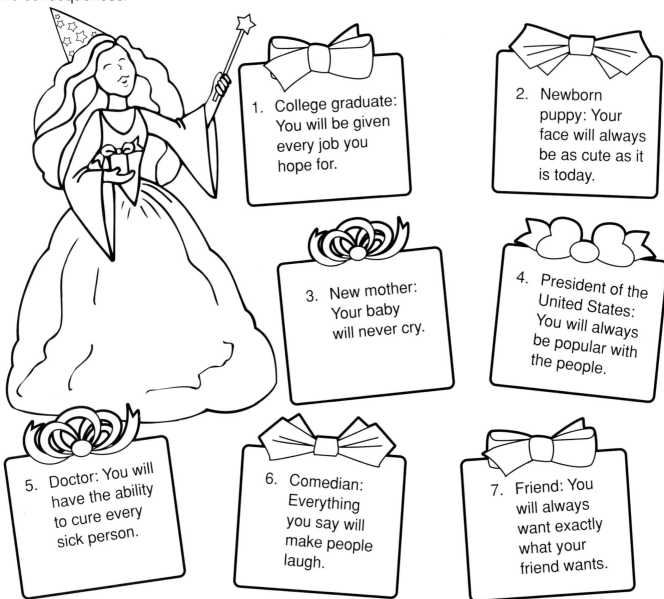

1. College graduate: You will be given every job you hope for.

2. Newborn puppy: Your face will always be as cute as it is today.

3. New mother: Your baby will never cry.

4. President of the United States: You will always be popular with the people.

5. Doctor: You will have the ability to cure every sick person.

6. Comedian: Everything you say will make people laugh.

7. Friend: You will always want exactly what your friend wants.

Think it through:

Consider gifts that Lucinda might give to each of the four people listed below. On a separate sheet of paper, draw four packages like the ones shown. Write the name of each person on the gift he or she will receive. Then describe the gift that Lucinda might give to that person.

1. astronaut ?

2. waitress ?

3. king ?

4. father ?

Fairy Tales

Ella's Enchanting Gift List

Part I Directions: Ella wants to begin her holiday shopping, but she is not sure how much money she will need. Help her determine how much each gift will cost by completing the chart below. Then help her find just the right gift or gifts for each person while staying within her budget.

Item	Silver KJs	Dollars
1. one dozen quail eggs	10	$60
2. meal in an inn (1 person)	1½	
3. one night's lodging		$42
4. silver chain and pendant	5	
5. *Creature Features Picture Dictionary*	2	
6. iron dragon cage		$87
7. dragon-shaped brass coal scuttle	5½	
8. centaur nut dish		$21
9. wolf's head stirrup cup	3	
10. CD of Ayorthaian songs	2½	
11. satin-stitch sewing machine		$102
12. *Illustrated Guide to Agulen Art*	6	
13. international coin collection kit		$27
14. furniture wax for banisters	½	
15. magic fairy book	8½	
16. "World's Best Godmother" mug	1	
17. enchanted throw rug		$57
18. silk scarf with red dragon	4	
19. *Languages for Beginners* (book and audiotape set)	6½	
20. "Elves and Fairies" computer game	8	
21. glass slippers (size 6)	7½	

Part II Directions: Help Ella find just the right gifts for three people on the list below. On the back of this sheet, show what she might buy for each person. Be sure that the amount spent on gifts for each person isn't more than the budgeted amount.

Person	Budget		Person	Budget
Mandy	15 KJs		Hattie	$30
Olive	$50		Char	25 KJs
Ella's children	35 KJs		Father	$110

Note to the teacher: Use with activity #9 on page 7.

Name____ *Ella Enchanted*

Ella in Disguise

An *anagram* is a word or phrase made from another word or phrase by scrambling the letters. For example, Ella hid behind a mask and disguised her name as Lela when she went to the ball.

Directions: Look at each of the boldfaced words in the sentences below. Scramble the letters to make a logical word to fill in each blank. **Hint:** Examples are shown on the ribbon around the page.

1. While Mandy stokes the **fires,** Ella enjoys ______________ with ketchup.
2. Ella found a **lump** in her ______________ pudding.
3. **Evil** ogres ______________ deep in the forest.
4. Ella almost didn't **dare** ______________ her book while on the trip.
5. Ella's heart **felt** heavy as she ______________ Char at the ball.
6. Mandy worked in the **kitchen,** waiting for the gravy to ______________.
7. Ella was **eager** to ______________ that she would marry the earl after eating elvish mushrooms.
8. Lucinda's **presents** were like poisonous ______________ to those who received them.
9. The prince looked **charming** when he was ______________ out of town in his uniform.
10. Mandy's **recipes** did not have ______________ ingredients.
11. After her mother's **death,** Ella ______________ to be without her.
12. It was a **miracle** that Ella was able to ______________ her ability to decide things for herself!
13. Finally, Ella **married** her longtime ______________.
14. When ogres **smile,** ______________ drips from their mouths.
15. It was hard for Ella to maintain her **dignity** when she had to do the washing and ______________.
16. Ella heard a **complaint** whenever she was not ______________.

sauce = cause
scent = cents
snake = sneak
notes = stone
spoon = snoop
step = pest
fare = fear
door = odor
name = mane
earn = near
grin = ring **grab = brag** **heat = hate** **lemon = melon**

 Note to the teacher: Use with activity #11 on page 7.

The Giver

by Lois Lowry

About the Book

In this book for mature readers, Jonas lives in a futuristic society. The community seems to be a *utopia,* a perfect place where there is neither warfare nor pain. There is food for everyone. There are no locked doors. And there are no choices.

When Jonas becomes 12, he is chosen to be the new Receiver of Memory. The Giver, who is to train Jonas for his life's work, begins to share with him the history of human experience: colors, warfare, and love. Jonas begins to realize that the tranquility of his home comes at a terrible price. That price includes killing. Escaping utopia, Jonas faces an uncertain future. But it is a future that he has chosen.

About the Author

Lois Lowry was born in Hawaii on March 20, 1937. Her father was an army dentist, so Lois moved often. She has lived all over the world, from New York to Pennsylvania, from Tokyo to Rhode Island. "I was a solitary child who lived in the world of books and my own imagination," says Lowry, the middle child of three.

Lowry's writing often deals with serious themes. Her first book, *A Summer to Die,* is a fictionalized story about the early death of her sister. In the books that have followed, Lowry has wrestled with issues such as the Holocaust, adoption, futuristic societies, and mental illness. She says that all of her books are essentially about human connections. Lowry has written more than 20 books and won the Newbery Medal twice, for *Number the Stars* and *The Giver.*

Student Contract Materials List

- Activity #1: copy of page 14
- Activity #2: copy of page 15, crayons or markers, thesaurus
- Activity #3: crayons or markers, ½ sheet of poster board, reference materials on modern inventions
- Activity #4: crayons or markers, 1 sheet of white paper
- Activity #5: samples of job applications
- Activity #6: crayons or markers, reference materials on health and nutrition

- Activity #7: paper, pencil
- Activity #8: copy of page 16
- Activity #9: crayons or markers
- Activity #10: paper, pencil
- Activity #11: crayons or markers, reference materials on the health benefits of bicycle riding
- Activity #12: arts-and-crafts supplies, reference materials on careers, shoebox

The Giver

Independent Contract

Name:_____ Number of activities to be completed: _____

1. Critical Thinking

One of the daily rituals for Jonas and his family is dealing with feelings after dinner each night. From small problems, such as those his sister Lily might encounter at school, to more serious ones, no emotion is too unimportant to discuss. During these discussions, Jonas and Lily's parents guide them toward understanding why people may act as they do. Obtain a copy of page 14 from your teacher to explore possible reasons for people's actions.

2. Language Arts

Jonas's best friend, Asher, is well known for his problems with imprecise speech. For example, during the Ceremony of Twelve, the Chief Elder tells a story about Asher mixing up the word *snack* with *smack* when he was a Three. Obtain a copy of page 15 from your teacher and practice precise speech.

3. Social Studies

Jonas and Lily live in a world very different from your own. For instance, they know little about animals or airplanes, things that are probably familiar to you. Make a list of ten modern conveniences that you and your friends might take for granted, such as air-conditioning and television. Using various reference materials, find out when each of the items on your list was invented. Then create a timeline that shows when these items were first made, illustrating and briefly describing each invention.

4. Language Arts

From the first three chapters of *The Giver,* what clues can you find that Jonas does not live in a society like yours? For example, one clue in the first few pages describes how a jet scares Jonas because jets are not allowed to fly over the community. (Today, it is not unusual for most Americans to see and hear planes.) Make a list of five clues from the book, and use them to write a brief description of where Jonas lives. After writing your description, illustrate his world.

5. Writing

Parents in Jonas's society have to fill out an application to get a child. After all, being a parent is a very important job! Read several job applications. Then make your own application for potential parents. Include questions that will determine what parenting skills an applicant has, how many hours a week the applicant is willing to spend parenting, and why the applicant wants the job. Next, present one of your parents with this application and have him or her fill it out. Discuss the results to discover your parent's special qualifications.

6. Science

The Giver mentions fish hatcheries in the community in which Jonas lives. There are, however, no references to cattle farms, chicken coops, or any other types of animals being used for food. From the book, it is safe to assume that fish are the community's main source of protein. Create a Fish Hatchery Attendant badge for yourself, and then research fish to find out their nutritional benefits. Write a short report about your findings on the back of the badge.

The Giver

Independent Contract

Name:_____ Number of activities to be completed: _____

7. Language Arts

Every morning Jonas and his family members share with one another whatever dreams they have had. For one week, write down your dreams each morning as soon as you wake. At the end of the week, choose the most vivid, most creative, or strangest dream to share. Tell your dream to your family and fellow students, and see if they can help you understand why you dreamed your dream.

8. Critical Thinking

In Jonas's society there are rules for everything. For example, all schoolchildren must volunteer in the community as part of their education. To discover some of these rules, obtain a copy of page 16 from your teacher to complete as directed.

9. Writing

Facing the harshness of the world outside of the community—being cold, hungry, and tired—Jonas wonders if it was a mistake to take Gabriel and choose freedom. Rewrite the ending of *The Giver*. Does Jonas give up his struggle and return to his community to face the consequences? Does he survive his struggle only to find another community just like the one he escaped? When you are through writing, add illustrations to your ending.

10. Social Studies

At the Ceremony of Twelve, each child is given a list of duties to perform daily. Reread chapter 9 to find the list of Jonas's duties as the community's new Receiver of Memories. Write a list of your daily duties at home and at school; then interview each family member to find out what he or she does. Compare your lists and see who does the most work in the family. Next, decide what each family member can do to lighten the others' loads and share the duties more evenly. Try your new duties for a week and see if it helps.

11. Science

Jonas, his friends, and even the adults in his community all ride bikes in their futuristic society. Although there is mention of buses and other vehicles, the majority of individual citizens rides bikes to and from work every day. Consult several health and fitness books and make a list of reasons why this type of transportation might be more healthful than our current practice of driving everywhere or taking the bus or subway. Prepare an attractive brochure or flyer promoting your findings, and present it to your class as a way to encourage class members and their families to use bikes more often.

12. Art

At the Ceremony of Twelve, all Twelves are assigned jobs they will have for the rest of their lives. Consult several career guides at your school or at the local library and decide what you might like to be when you grow up. Create a model of your future office or workplace. Without labeling it, see if your classmates can tell what you want to be when you grow up!

The Other Side of the Coin

Directions: Lily's family helps her deal with her anger at a boy by asking her to try to understand his actions: What might the boy have been feeling at the time that made him act the way he did? On the coins below you will find a variety of actions a person might take. On the other side of the coin, write a possible explanation for why someone might act that way. The first one has been done for you.

At lunch, Harriet steals April's carton of milk.

___Harriet___ ___forgot her___ ___lunch money___ ___and was___ ___embarrassed.___

In class, Richard always asks the teacher to repeat herself.

During silent reading, Sally always falls asleep.

Robby is late to school two or three mornings per week.

After school, Bobby pushes Damon down.

Monica keeps forgetting her permission slip for the field trip.

Phil asks to go to the bathroom before every quiz.

Billy always gets a stomach-ache just before P.E.

At recess, Keisha cuts in front of the line to play kick ball.

Note to the teacher: Use with activity #1 on page 12.

Appropriate Adjectives

Part I Directions: Precise language is an important theme in *The Giver.* Jonas corrects himself at one point when he says, "It was too strong an adjective." Practice preciseness by circling the most appropriate adjectives in the sentences below. The first one has been done for you.

1. I got distraught/distracted watching the garbagemen and was late for school.

2. The movie starting ten minutes late was really tragic/inconvenient.

3. That story made me sad/depressed.

4. It wasn't that hard to jump across the big/vast ditch.

5. Jumping rope for five minutes sure makes you tired/exhausted!

6. After walking for half an hour, Brian was dehydrated/thirsty.

7. Having a sunburn is always annoying/traumatic.

8. I had only two slices of pizza! I'm still hungry/starving!

9. The bruise on my arm is unsightly/revolting.

10. The baby's laughter was loud/deafening.

11. The TV movie was scary/petrifying.

12. The Sunday paper is always large/massive.

13. The low attendance at the car wash was disappointing/disastrous.

14. Reading out loud in class can be nerve-racking/petrifying.

15. The class pizza party was fun/stupendous!

I want my snack!

Part II Directions:
Make a list of ten simple words like *hungry, big,* and *tired.* Then, using a thesaurus, find words with similar but exaggerated meanings, such as *starving, whopping,* and *bushed.* Next, choose five sets of similar words and make simple drawings of each word. For example, an illustration of *hungry* would be quite different from an illustration of *starving.*

Note to the teacher: Use with activity #2 on page 12.

Reading for Rules

Attention.
This is a
reminder....

Directions: Use the following quotes from *The Giver* to compile a list of rules for the society in which Jonas lives. Be sure to be specific when writing your list of rules. The first one has been done for you.

Quotes

1. "Two children—one male, one female—to each family unit."

2. "This evening he almost would have preferred to keep his feelings hidden. But it was, of course, against the rules."

3. "…and when you're an Eight, your comfort object will be taken away."

4. "THIS IS A REMINDER TO FEMALES UNDER NINE THAT HAIR RIBBONS ARE TO BE NEATLY TIED AT ALL TIMES."

5. "There was never any comfortable way to mention or discuss one's successes without breaking the rule against bragging.…"

6. "I'd been teaching her to ride [my bike], even though technically I wasn't supposed to."

7. "No doors in the community were locked, ever."

8. "What if they were allowed to choose their own mate?"

9. "He glanced quickly at the wall speaker, terrified that the Committee might be listening as they could at any time."

Rules

1. You will have only two children per family unit: one male and one female.

2. _____

3. _____

4. _____

5. _____

6. _____

7. _____

8. _____

9. _____

©2001 The Education Center, Inc. • *Contracts for Independent Readers* • Fantasy • TEC791 • Key p. 62

16   **Note to the teacher:** Use with activity #8 on page 13.

Harry Potter and the Sorcerer's Stone
by J. K. Rowling

About the Book

Harry Potter has lived his entire life with his aunt, uncle, and cousin Dudley. Harry sleeps in a cupboard under the stairs, wears Dudley's cast-off clothing, and has never had a birthday party. His aunt and uncle regard him as a great nuisance and waste no time or affection on him. In fact, they try to pretend he doesn't exist. One day Harry learns that he is a wizard and that he will attend Hogwarts School of Witchcraft and Wizardry. At Hogwarts, Harry is invited to join the Quidditch team and, for the first time in his life, makes friends. Unfortunately, certain aspects of Harry's new life aren't so wonderful, such as the way Professor Snape, the House of Slytherin, and Lord Voldemort all seem to want to see the end of Harry Potter.

About the Author

Joanne Kathleen (J. K.) Rowling was born on July 31, 1965, in Gloucestershire, England. She began writing at the age of six when she wrote her first story, "Rabbit," because she and her sister had always wanted a rabbit. Joanne always told stories to her younger sister and her friends.

At Exeter University, Rowling followed her parents' advice to major in French so that she could become a bilingual secretary. She says this was a big mistake. She calls herself "the worst secretary ever." When she should have been taking notes in meetings, she was writing stories instead. Rowling left the secretarial profession and moved to Portugal to teach English as a foreign language. She loved teaching English, which she taught in the afternoons and evenings, giving her the mornings to write. This is when she began writing *Harry Potter and the Sorcerer's Stone* (known in the United Kingdom as *Harry Potter and the Philosopher's Stone*).

Rowling now lives in Edinburgh, Scotland, with her daughter. It took a year for a publisher to buy the first Harry Potter book, but now she has enough money to quit teaching and write full time. She even has her own rabbit!

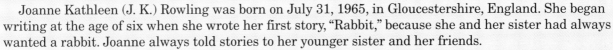

Student Contract Materials List

- Activity #1:   white drawing paper, crayons or markers
- Activity #2:   white drawing paper, crayons or markers
- Activity #3:   construction paper, crayons or markers, arts-and-crafts supplies, glue, scissors
- Activity #4:   paper, pencil
- Activity #5:   reference materials on Great Britain, ½ sheet of poster board, crayons or markers
- Activity #6:   copy of page 20

- Activity #7:   white paper, tea bag, newspapers, calligraphy pen, calligraphy books or lettering guides
- Activity #8:   household items, arts-and-crafts supplies, glue, scissors, markers
- Activity #9:   1 sheet of newsprint, crayons or markers
- Activity #10: shoebox, craft supplies, 2 index cards, tape
- Activity #11: chess set, instructions for playing chess
- Activity #12: copy of page 21

Harry Potter and the Sorcerer's Stone

Independent Contract

Name:_____ Number of activities to be completed: _____

1. Language Arts

Hogwarts School of Witchcraft and Wizardry has a long and prestigious history of providing training to witches and wizards. Create an informational brochure to advertise Hogwarts. Include a description of the program and staff, an introduction to the four houses, and a preview of some of the special programs at the school, such as Quidditch. Also include information from the story, such as a supplies list, the school song, and faculty members' names, followed by the courses they teach. Decorate the brochure's cover with an original Hogwarts school emblem and other illustrations.

2. Art

Harry has some magical tools for wizards only, such as his cloak of invisibility and his Nimbus Two Thousand flying broom. If you could choose one of these wizard tools to use for a day, which one would you choose? Create a comic strip starring yourself and one of the tools. Include details about where you go, what you do, and whom you see. Do you rescue someone or save the world from evil villains?

3. Language Arts

A movie about Harry Potter is going to be made, and you are in charge of making a commercial to advertise it. Think about which scenes from the story would be exciting to see. Choose one scene and write a script for it. Then make or provide the props you will need. Cast yourself and other class members in the parts. Practice and then perform your commercial for the class.

4. Language Arts

Lots of things would take getting used to if you were to move from the Muggle world to the wizard world, and vice versa. Compare these two worlds by making a table. Label the rows with at least ten different aspects of these two worlds, such as celebrity trading cards, transportation, food, pets, banks, and clothing. Label the columns "Muggle World" and "Wizard World." Then, in each row, write a description or draw a picture to illustrate the differences in the worlds. Write the page number for each fact from the story next to the corresponding fact in the table.

5. Social Studies

J. K. Rowling, the author of the Harry Potter series, lives in Edinburgh, Scotland, and Harry Potter's imaginary world is set in Great Britain. Research Great Britain and the cultures of the people who live there. Make a Great Britain poster, including a map that shows the political divisions, at least six major cities, and at least six historical sites you would like to visit. Around the poster, provide factual information and pictures about the places marked on the map, and include other interesting information, such as the different countries' flags, monies, and governments.

6. Math

Muggle money is familiar to Harry, but wizard money is a new and curious currency to him. Harry gets some practice using the new money when he purchases his school supplies. Obtain a copy of page 20 from your teacher and practice using wizard money.

©2001 The Education Center, Inc. • *Contracts for Independent Readers • Fantasy* • TEC791

Harry Potter and the Sorcerer's Stone
Independent Contract

Name:_____ Number of activities to be completed: _____

 Art

At Hogwarts, the students write on parchment paper using quills and ink. Make your own parchment paper by laying a sheet of paper on a stack of newspapers. Wet a tea bag and gently dab it over the paper to give it a tan background. Allow the paper to dry. Using a calligraphy pen, practice writing letters on scrap paper. Then write the Mirror of Erised's inscription from chapter 12 on the top half of your parchment paper. On the bottom half, write what you think the inscription means based on what Dumbledore shows each person.

 Language Arts

Create a curiosity collection for *Harry Potter and the Sorcerer's Stone*. Make a list of 15 items from the story that could be used to tell about a character, place, or event. Then find or make the objects to put in your collection. For example, a stuffed toy owl could represent Hedwig, a new cover on a paperback book could become a Hogwarts textbook, or a sorting hat could be made out of decorated felt or poster board. Share your collection with the class, explaining what each item is and its importance in the book.

 Writing

The *Daily Prophet* is not an ordinary newspaper. It is written by witches and wizards. Design the front page of the next *Daily Prophet*. Include articles about Hogwarts, an update on Gringotts, and several other interesting articles. Also include ads for wizard products and establishments.

 Art

The wizard world is vastly different from the Muggle world. Illustrate the differences in these two worlds by making a diorama. Think about places that Harry visits and sees, such as his aunt and uncle's house, the train station, and the stores where he buys his school supplies. Divide a shoebox in half. In one half create a Muggle scene, and in the other half create a wizard scene. On separate index cards, write a description for each half of the box. Tape the cards to the bottom front edge of the box in front of their matching scenes.

 Critical Thinking

Checkmate! The stakes are high in the game of wizard chess. Challenge a knight and you may end up the victim of a sword wound! Obtain a copy of the instructions for real chess and write a summary of them. Make a list of each of the pieces, and write a description of the type of move each piece can make. Play the game by yourself to practice the different moves. Then challenge a friend to a game!

 Critical Thinking

As Harry, Ron, and Hermione set forth to find the Sorcerer's Stone, they face a number of challenges. Not all of these challenges require the use of spells or magical powers. Some are skill, logic, and critical-thinking puzzles. Review the seven challenges that Harry and his friends face in their quest for the stone in chapters 16 and 17. Then obtain a copy of page 21 from your teacher and use logic to solve each problem.

Wizard Wealth

Harry is faced with trying to use wizard money when he isn't used to it yet. Follow the directions below to help Harry solve his money problems.

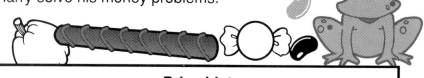

Directions: Read the conversion table and price list. Then use them to solve each problem.

Conversion Table
1 Galleon	=	17 Sickles
1 Sickle	=	29 Knuts

Price List
Bertie Bott's Every Flavor Beans	3 Knuts per scoop
Drooble's Best Blowing Gum	6 Knuts
Chocolate Frog	1 Sickle
Pumpkin Pasty	20 Knuts
Licorice Wand	15 Knuts
Cauldron Cake	2 Sickles
Nimbus Two Thousand	50 Galleons
Daily Prophet Newspaper	1 Galleon

1. How many Sickles would it cost to buy a *Daily Prophet* newspaper? _____

2. What would your change be if you paid for 1 Pumpkin Pasty with a gold Galleon? _____
   _____

3. About how many scoops of Every Flavor Beans could you buy for 1 Galleon? _____

4. Which would cost less: 3 Chocolate Frogs or 15 pieces of Drooble's Best Blowing Gum? ___
   _____

5. You have 48 Galleons and 5 Sickles. How much more do you need to buy a Nimbus Two Thousand? _____

6. If there are 20 beans per scoop, how much would 100 Every Flavor Beans cost? _____
   _____

7. How much more would 4 Licorice Wands cost than a Chocolate Frog? _____

8. If Harry has 800 Sickles and 1,942 Knuts and he wants to buy a new Nimbus Two Thousand and a *Daily Prophet* newspaper, does he have enough money? Why or why not? _____
   _____

9. If Harry has 4 Sickles left and he wants to buy Ron one of each treat on the list, does he have enough money? Why or why not? _____

10. On the Express to Hogwarts, Harry bought some of everything from the snack cart. If he bought 20 scoops of Every Flavor Beans, 5 pieces of Best Blowing Gum, 3 Chocolate Frogs, 2 Pumpkin Pasties, 2 Cauldron Cakes, and 5 Licorice Wands, how much did he spend?
    _____

Note to the teacher: Use with activity #6 on page 18.

Name _____

Peculiar Puzzles

Directions: Use logic to solve the puzzles below.

I. Color each potion the color indicated. Read the rhyming clues to help you determine which magical potion you should choose. Then circle the safe potion.

From the bottle with a handle you'd enjoy a few sweet sips, but next to it are poisons, so don't let them touch your lips.

The yellow stuff that tastes so good is a lemon brew, but even though it's sweet to drink, it will turn you into stew.

Avoid the steaming concoction and the colored potion it matches, and he who drinks the boiling red will be covered with itchy patches.

Good luck, my friend, in your puzzling search—I hope you will not cower; now choose the potion to safely drink that will give you magical power!

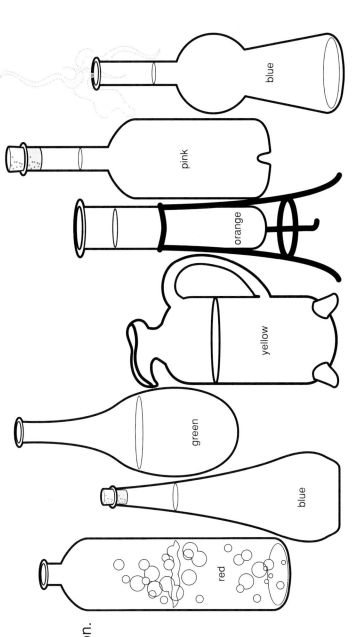

blue

pink

orange

yellow

green

blue

red

II. Choose the key that fits the lock—the wings provide the clues; so study hard, think carefully, and then you'll have to choose! Circle the key you've chosen.

Ignore the keys with double wings for they will not unlock a thing.

Wings with spots may be of use, but the slenderest wings will only confuse.

The matching keys are a curious pair, for though one works, leave the other there.

A bat wing won't help you win, but one that is near it will let you in.

The wing of feathers will not alight, but the desired key is to its upper right.

The rhyme has ended; there is no more. Now choose the key that unlocks the door!

Note to the teacher: Use with activity #12 on page 19.

21

The Lion, the Witch and the Wardrobe
by C. S. Lewis

About the Book

When Peter, Susan, Edmund, and Lucy are sent to live with an old professor in his mysterious house, they have no idea what adventures await them. One day while investigating one of the many rooms, Lucy opens the door to a wardrobe and steps inside. To her surprise she walks into another world entirely—Narnia. Unfortunately, when Lucy returns, no one believes the story of her adventure. But it's not long before all four children find themselves in Narnia in the midst of a conflict between good and evil. They realize that they will need the help of Aslan, the great Lion, to triumph over the White Witch, who has made it always winter.

About the Author

C. S. Lewis was born in Belfast, Ireland, in 1898. Growing up, nearly every room in his house was filled with books. He read one after another. When his older brother was sent to boarding school, Lewis spent much of his time in the attic writing stories and illustrating them. He liked to write about animals suited in armor.

After the death of his mother, Lewis joined his brother at the boarding school in England. Later, he taught English Literature at Magdalen College, Oxford, from 1925 to 1954 and at Cambridge University from 1954 to 1963. Lewis wrote more than 50 books, most of which were religious books for adults. It's estimated that 100 million copies of his books have been sold. He died in 1963.

Lewis gave the following advice to aspiring writers: turn off the radio, read all the good books you can, write with your ear and not your eye, and write about what interests you.

Student Contract Materials List

- Activity #1: crayons or colored pencils, white paper
- Activity #2: 12" x 18" construction paper, crayons or markers, dictionary, scissors, scrap paper, glue
- Activity #3: four 3" x 5" index cards, hole puncher, recipe, ribbon
- Activity #4: 12" x 18" black construction paper, white crayon or colored chalk
- Activity #5: reference materials on trees and flowers
- Activity #6: copy of page 25, dictionary or encyclopedias

- Activity #7: markers, poster board, reference materials on lions
- Activity #8: reference materials on England
- Activity #9: copy of page 26, dictionary or thesaurus
- Activity #10: 12" x 18" light-colored construction paper, crayons or markers
- Activity #11: 9" x 12" construction paper, crayons or markers
- Activity #12: coat hanger, 9" x 12" construction paper, crayons or markers, scissors, tape, string

The Lion, the Witch and the Wardrobe
Independent Contract

Name:_____ Number of activities to be completed: _____

1. Art

When Lucy returns from her first visit to Narnia, her brothers and sister believe that she made up her adventure. Help Lucy convince them that this land exists by designing a travel brochure featuring Narnia as a vacation destination. Fold a sheet of drawing paper into thirds so that the sections overlap. Design and draw an eye-catching outer flap that invites the reader to visit. On the inner flap create a nickname for Narnia. Finally, on the three inside sections, advertise and illustrate the following features: "Places to Visit," "Things to See," and "People to Meet."

2. Reading

Construct a wardrobe by folding a sheet of construction paper so that the two ends meet in the middle, forming two doors. Add top and bottom trim to the wardrobe using scrap paper, and then decorate it to look like the picture in chapter 1. Cut out a lamppost shape and glue it to the inside center of the wardrobe. Write each word listed below inside the wardrobe. Look up each word in a dictionary. Under each word, write its definition.

chap	looking-glass	row	wireless
wardrobe	blue-bottle	sledge	beastly
trifle	larder		

3. Writing

During Edmund's visit to Narnia, the White Witch magically creates Turkish Delight for him. Edmund, not knowing that whoever eats enchanted food will want more and more, eats the sweets. What food do you find enchanting? Describe the delicacy on four index cards by following the directions below. When completed, punch a hole in the upper left-hand corner of each card and tie them together with ribbon.

Card #1: Title your recipe "[Your name]'s Delight: A Royal Recipe." Decorate the card.
Card #2: List the major ingredients.
Card #3: Write the directions for making it.
Card #4: Describe why this food is so enchanting.

4. Reading

Peter, Susan, Edmund, and Lucy meet many creatures during their adventures in Narnia. Some of these creatures are good and some are evil. Divide a sheet of construction paper in half; title one side "Good" and the other side "Evil." Then record the names of ten creatures the children encounter on their journey and list them in either the "Good" or the "Evil" column (five creatures in each column). Next to each name write a short phrase describing that creature. Finally, decorate the outer portion of each side seasonally: the evil side with winter-related items, the good side with spring-related items.

5. Science

As spring returns to Narnia, nature comes to life again. Research each type of tree or flower below that's mentioned in chapters 11 and 12. Then create a Narnian nature crossword puzzle using the words below and your researched facts as clues.

fir	oak	elm	beech
hawthorn	laburnum	larch	birch
celandine	crocus	primrose	bluebell

6. Research

Mythical creatures are popular residents of Narnia. Obtain a copy of page 25 from your teacher and learn more about these mysterious beings.

The Lion, the Witch and the Wardrobe
Independent Contract

Name:_____ Number of activities to be completed: _____

7. Science

In Narnia, the Lion, Aslan, is known as the King and the Lord of the whole wood. In our world, the lion is often called the king of beasts. Create a web presenting facts about lions. In the center, draw a castle and title the web "The King of Beasts." Draw lines extending outward from the castle to four thrones containing the following titles: "The King's Appearance," "The King's Home," "The King's Hunting," and "The King's Cubs." Research two or three facts in each category and record the information inside the corresponding throne shape.

8. Social Studies

In *The Lion, the Witch and the Wardrobe* the old professor's house is an attraction for sightseers in England. Pretend that you are traveling to England. While you are there, you want to visit some famous attractions. After researching places of interest in England, make a list of the top five sight-seeing spots you would include in your trip. Next to each spot, describe the location and why you want to visit the attraction.

9. Language Arts

C. S. Lewis uses many descriptive words in *The Lion, the Witch and the Wardrobe*. He uses some words that expand young readers' vocabularies. Obtain a copy of page 26 from your teacher and help expand your vocabulary.

10. Writing

After being crowned kings and queens of Narnia, time passes and the children become known as King Peter the Magnificent, Queen Susan the Gentle, King Edmund the Just, and Queen Lucy the Valiant. Draw a large royal shield. Divide the shield into four sections. Write a different royal name across the top of each section and the corresponding descriptive word vertically down the left side. For example, you would write "Queen Lucy" across the top and "Valiant" down the side. For each character, write phrases describing that character beginning with each letter of the descriptive word to create an acrostic poem.

11. Art

Honors and rewards are given to the friends of Peter, Susan, Edmund, and Lucy for their help in overthrowing the White Witch. Design an award for Mr. Tumnus, the Beavers, Giant Rumblebuffin, or the leopards. On the award include to whom the award is being given, what quality was exhibited, a specific example of where this quality was demonstrated, and who is giving the award. Think of someone you know who has exhibited this same quality and also make an award for him or her.

12. Writing

Peter, Susan, Edmund, and Lucy hunt the White Stag, who will give wishes to whomever catches it. What kind of things would you wish for if you were able to catch the White Stag? Design a mobile with your wishes. Draw and cut out a white, male deer and write the title "White Stag Wishes" on it. Tape the deer along the top of a hanger. Then draw and cut out nine hunting horns and hang them from the hanger. On the horns, write three wishes for each of the following: yourself, your family, and the world.

©2001 The Education Center, Inc. • *Contracts for Independent Readers • Fantasy* • TEC791

Creature Clue Crowns

Each crown contains clues about a mythical creature found in Narnia. Read the clues and pick the creature's name from the word box. Write the word in the crown's band. You may use a dictionary or encyclopedias to help you "crown" the creatures.

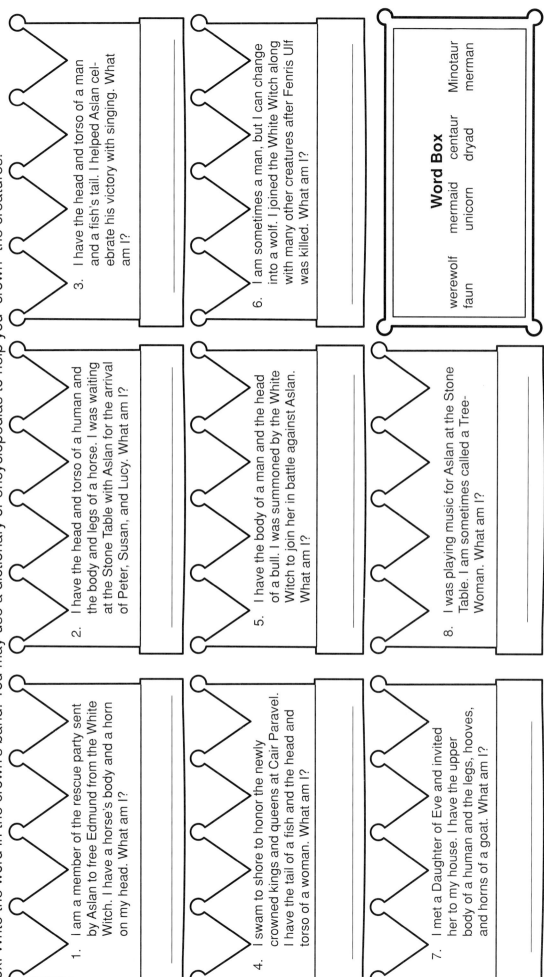

1. I am a member of the rescue party sent by Aslan to free Edmund from the White Witch. I have a horse's body and a horn on my head. What am I?

2. I have the head and torso of a human and the body and legs of a horse. I was waiting at the Stone Table with Aslan for the arrival of Peter, Susan, and Lucy. What am I?

3. I have the head and torso of a man and a fish's tail. I helped Aslan celebrate his victory with singing. What am I?

4. I swam to shore to honor the newly crowned kings and queens at Cair Paravel. I have the tail of a fish and the head and torso of a woman. What am I?

5. I have the body of a man and the head of a bull. I was summoned by the White Witch to join her in battle against Aslan. What am I?

6. I am sometimes a man, but I can change into a wolf. I joined the White Witch along with many other creatures after Fenris Ulf was killed. What am I?

7. I met a Daughter of Eve and invited her to my house. I have the upper body of a human and the legs, hooves, and horns of a goat. What am I?

8. I was playing music for Aslan at the Stone Table. I am sometimes called a Tree-Woman. What am I?

Word Box

werewolf	mermaid	centaur	Minotaur
faun	unicorn	dryad	merman

©2001 The Education Center, Inc. • Contracts for Independent Readers • Fantasy • TEC791 • Key p. 63

Note to the teacher: Use with activity #6 on page 23.

Name _____

Stone Table Synonyms

The words below are from *The Lion, the Witch and the Wardrobe.* Look up each word in a dictionary or thesaurus. Write the matching synonym from the Stone Table on the blank beside each word.

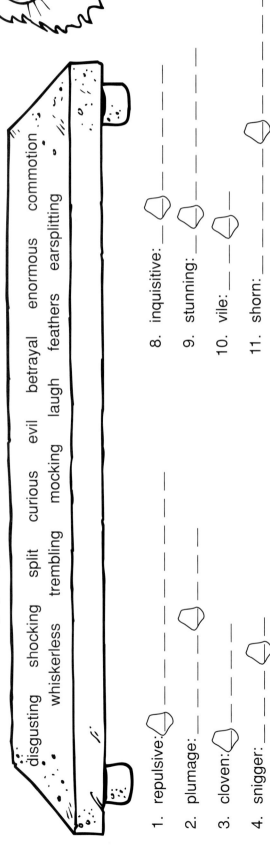

| disgusting | shocking | split | curious | evil | betrayal | enormous | commotion |
| whiskerless | | trembling | mocking | laugh | feathers | earsplitting |

1. repulsive: _ _ _ _ _

2. plumage: _ _ _ _ _

3. cloven: _ _ _ _ _

4. snigger: _ _ _ _ _

5. prodigious: _ _ _ _ _

6. bustle: _ _ _ _ _

7. deafening: _ _ _ _ _

8. inquisitive: _ _ _ _ _

9. stunning: _ _ _ _ _

10. vile: _ _ _ _ _

11. shorn: _ _ _ _ _

12. quivering: _ _ _ _ _

13. jeering: _ _ _ _ _

14. treachery: _ _ _ _ _

Unscramble the circled letters to discover why Edmund betrayed his brother and sisters. Write the reason for Edmund's treachery on the stones below.

Note to the teacher: Use with activity #9 on page 24.

Matilda
by Roald Dahl

About the Book

When an extremely exceptional child like Matilda is born to extremely awful parents like the Wormwoods, something is bound to happen! And it does! Matilda has read all of the children's books in the public library and has started her way through classics such as Charles Dickens's *Great Expectations*. She also discovers that she has the unusual ability to move objects with her mind. This ability combined with her amazing intelligence gets Matilda into lots of trouble, usually at the expense of her pathetic parents or the horrible headmistress, Miss Trunchbull.

About the Author

Roald Dahl was born on September 13, 1916, in Llandaff, South Wales. He was a fun-loving, mischievous child. His father died when he was four and his mother kept his father's wish that he attend English schools. Roald attended Llandaff Cathedral School, then boarding school at St. Peters, and finally Repton Private School. Roald was never a superior student.

After his schooling, Dahl chose to work for the Shell Oil Company in Africa rather than go on to college. In 1939, he joined the Royal Air Force, serving first as a pilot and later as an assistant air attaché in Washington, D.C. During this time he was interviewed by the *Saturday Evening Post*. The interviewer didn't take notes, so he picked up Dahl's notes, which were actually a story. The interviewer sent the story to the magazine and started Dahl on his way to becoming a writer, which Dahl later called a complete fluke. His first children's book was called *The Gremlins*. Later, Dahl made up bedtime stories for his five children, learning from them what children like. He kept their interest by throwing in unexpected twists. This technique became characteristic of the work of Roald Dahl, one of the best-known authors of humorous books for children.

Student Contract Materials List

- Activity #1: first-day-of-school photos, 5 sheets of white paper, glue, crayons or markers
- Activity #2: copy of page 30, crayons or markers
- Activity #3: 1 book or 1 movie based on a book by Roald Dahl
- Activity #4: 1 sheet of construction paper, 5 sheets of white paper, crayons or markers, stapler
- Activity #5: paper, pencil
- Activity #6: paper, pencil
- Activity #7: copy of page 31
- Activity #8: white paper, crayons or markers
- Activity #9: white paper, highlighter, dictionary
- Activity #10: 2 sheets of white paper, scissors, stapler
- Activity #11: copy of page 32, access to a public library
- Activity #12: reference materials on telekinesis

Matilda
Independent Contract

Name:_____ Number of activities to be completed: _____

1. Writing

Matilda's first day of school is memorable for her. Think back to your very first day of school. Whom did you meet for the first time? Do you still know anyone from that class? What were your classroom and teacher like? What would you change about that first day if you could go back? Answer these four questions to create a photo essay. For each question, glue a photo or draw a picture of the answer on a different sheet of paper. Underneath each picture, write a short paragraph giving details about the picture and your first day. Design a cover; then staple the pages together to make a booklet.

2. Reading

Matilda is definitely a misunderstood child! Many things happen in her life that only she can explain. Obtain a copy of page 30 from your teacher and find out the stories behind the events.

3. Language Arts

There are many similar characteristics among Roald Dahl's books for children. Either read or watch a video of another Roald Dahl story, such as *Willie Wonka and the Chocolate Factory, James and the Giant Peach, The BFG,* or *Danny the Champion of the World.* Then, on a sheet of paper, draw a T chart. Label one side *Matilda* and the other side with the title of the other story. List the stories' similarities, including information on the child characters, the grown-up characters, the plot, the setting, the problem, and how the child character solves the problem.

4. Writing

Imagine that Mr. and Mrs. Wormwood write a book called "How to Be a Horrible Parent in 10 Easy Steps." What would be included in it? Fold five sheets of paper in half. At the top of each of the ten pages, write a tip from the Wormwoods on how to be the worst parent possible. Use events from the book as examples. Illustrate each page with a picture demonstrating the tip. Fold, decorate, and title a sheet of construction paper to make a cover. Insert the pages inside the cover; then staple along the fold to complete your book.

5. Math

Matilda is able to solve difficult math problems in her head. Write an addition, subtraction, multiplication, or division problem at the top of a sheet of paper. At the bottom, draw a picture of Matilda. Draw thought bubbles around her. In each bubble write one of the steps needed to solve the problem. For example: 3,456 + 4,689. Step 1: Add 6 and 9 to get 15. Write the 5 in the ones column below the problem and write the 1 in the tens column above the problem. Make sure you give the correct answer in the last bubble!

6. Writing

A diamante is a poem that can be used to compare two different people or things. Follow the guidelines below to write a diamante comparing Matilda to one other character.
Line 1: Name (Matilda)
Line 2: Two adjectives describing Matilda
Line 3: Three -ing verbs describing Matilda
Line 4: Two nouns describing Matilda and two nouns describing the other character
Line 5: Three -ing verbs describing the other character
Line 6: Two adjectives describing the other character
Line 7: The other character's name

Matilda
Independent Contract

Name:_____ Number of activities to be completed: _____

 ### 7. Critical Thinking

The characters in *Matilda* are very colorful, and some have exaggerated traits. Obtain a copy of page 31 from your teacher and learn more about the traits of some of these characters.

 ### 8. Math

Roald Dahl wrote many books for children, some of which have been made into movies. Which of Dahl's stories do your friends like the most? Prepare a survey listing at least five of Dahl's stories, such as *Charlie and the Chocolate Factory, The Witches, The BFG,* and *Boy.* Ask each classmate to choose his or her favorite story from the list. After you have collected the data, prepare a bar graph showing the results of the survey. Share the results with your class.

 ### 9. Language Arts

What characteristics does *Matilda* have that make it a fantasy? Look up the definition of fantasy. Then find the plot, the setting, the main characters, and the problem and solution in the story. What aspects of fantasy can you find in each of these story elements? Fold a sheet of paper in half and then fold it in half again. Unfold the paper and label each of the four sections with the story elements listed above. Then list the information you find in the appropriate squares. Highlight each piece of information that helps prove that *Matilda* is a fantasy novel.

10. Language Arts

Pretend that you are a detective investigating the disappearance of Miss Trunchbull. Cut two pieces of paper in half vertically and staple the top edges together to make a detective's notebook. Then pretend to interview at least three characters from *Matilda* to find out the facts leading to the disappearance. In your notebook, write down the name of each person who supplies an eyewitness account and a description of the event. For example, "Matilda: Miss Trunchbull fainted in class after yelling at all of us." On the last page of the notebook, write your solution to Miss Trunchbull's disappearance based on these clues.

 ### 11. Research

One of Matilda's favorite places is the library. Here she learns to love some really great books. Obtain a copy of page 32 from your teacher. Then take a trip to your public library and learn more about some of Matilda's favorites.

 ### 12. Research

Matilda is able to move things just by thinking about them. This is called *telekinesis* (*tele* = distance; *kinesis* = moving), or moving things from a distance. Use reference materials to research telekinesis. Do you think telekinesis is really possible? Why or why not? How could you prove or disprove it scientifically? Write a letter to Roald Dahl explaining why you do or do not believe telekinesis is possible.

Behind the Scenes

When unusual things occur in the book, Matilda usually knows what's going on behind the scenes. Read each sentence starter below. Complete each sentence with what Matilda knew. Then draw a picture showing Matilda's role in the event.

1. Mrs. Phelps thinks *Great Expectations* might be too long for me, but I know that I _____ _____ _____ _____	2. Daddy thinks *The Red Pony* is "filth" and starts tearing it up, but I know that he _____ _____ _____ _____	3. Mommy thinks Daddy grabbed the wrong bottle when he bleached his hair, but I know _____ _____ _____	4. Miss Trunchbull thinks that I am the one who tipped over the glass with the newt in it. I told her I haven't left my desk, but I know _____ _____ _____ _____
5. Daddy thinks I cheated when I figured out the profit on the cars he sold, but I know that he _____ _____ _____ _____	6. Miss Honey thinks that she will never get her house back, but I know _____ _____	7. Miss Trunchbull thinks the ghost of Magnus has come to haunt her, but I know _____ _____ _____	8. Miss Honey doesn't believe my parents will give me up so I can live with her, but I know _____ _____ _____ _____

Note to the teacher: Use with activity #2 on page 28.

WANTED!

The characters from *Matilda* are wanted for questioning. Complete each wanted poster below by drawing a picture of the wanted person and filling in the appropriate information from the book.

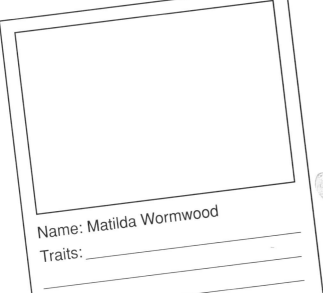

Name: Matilda Wormwood

Traits: _____

_____

Goal: _____

_____

Name: Miss Jennifer Honey

Traits: _____

_____

Goal: _____

_____

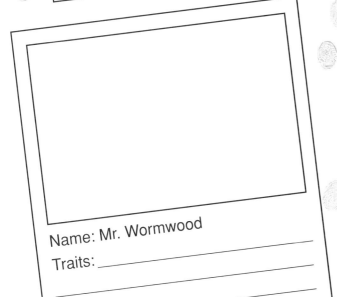

Name: Mr. Wormwood

Traits: _____

_____

Goal: _____

_____

Name: Miss Agatha Trunchbull

Traits: _____

_____

Goal: _____

_____

Book Lovers' Delight

Part I: The cards below give details about some of Matilda's favorite books. Go to your public library and find these books. Read one page out of each book. Then on each card write your opinion of the interest level, the style, or something you learned from the book.

1. Title: *Nicholas Nickleby*
   Author: Charles Dickens
   Opinion: _____
   _____
   _____

2. Title: *Jane Eyre*
   Author: Charlotte Brontë
   Opinion: _____
   _____
   _____

3. Title: *Pride and Prejudice*
   Author: Jane Austen
   Opinion: _____
   _____
   _____

4. Title: *Gone to Earth*
   Author: Mary Webb
   Opinion: _____
   _____
   _____

5. Title: *The Old Man and the Sea*
   Author: Ernest Hemingway
   Opinion: _____
   _____
   _____

6. Title: *The Grapes of Wrath*
   Author: John Steinbeck
   Opinion: _____
   _____
   _____

7. Title: *Kim*
   Author: Rudyard Kipling
   Opinion: _____
   _____
   _____

8. Title: *The Sound and the Fury*
   Author: William Faulkner
   Opinion: _____
   _____
   _____

Part II: Think about four-year-old Matilda reading the books listed above. Do you think it is possible for a four-year-old to read these books? Why or why not? _____
_____

Note to the teacher: Use with activity #11 on page 29.

Mrs. Frisby and the Rats of NIMH
by Robert C. O'Brien

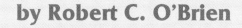

About the Book

Mrs. Frisby, a widowed mouse with four small children, is faced with a problem. She must move her family to its summer quarters immediately, or they will be destroyed by a farmer during his spring plowing. Mrs. Frisby's youngest son, Timothy, is ill with pneumonia and cannot get out of bed. While seeking help, Mrs. Frisby has many adventures, including slipping sleeping powder into a ferocious cat's dinner and flying on the back of a crow. Fortunately, she is able to enlist the aid of the rats of NIMH, an extraordinary breed of highly intelligent creatures, who come up with a plan to save the Frisby house and family.

About the Author

Robert C. O'Brien is the pen name for Robert Leslie Conly. Robert was born on January 11, 1918, in Brooklyn, New York, but grew up mainly on Long Island, New York. As a child, Robert showed musical talent. He would eventually study at the Juilliard School of Music and later the Eastman School of the University of Rochester, where he also earned a degree in English.

O'Brien spent most of his life writing in one form or another. He wrote for *Newsweek* and other maga-

zines and newspapers until 1951, when he joined the staff of *National Geographic* magazine. O'Brien had many interests, including music, reading, furniture making, and nature. He didn't begin writing fiction until the last ten years of his life. He chose to write under a pen name because *National Geographic* frowned on its staff publishing any outside writing. O'Brien had a wife, a son, and three daughters. Until his death on March 5, 1973, it was not generally known that Robert C. O'Brien, fiction writer, and Robert L. Conly, senior assistant editor of *National Geographic* magazine, were one and the same.

Student Contract Materials List

- Activity #1:   socks, markers, arts-and-crafts supplies
- Activity #2:   paper, pencil
- Activity #3:   reference materials on animal habitats, white drawing paper, colored pencils
- Activity #4:   paper, pencil
- Activity #5:   copy of page 36
- Activity #6:   reference materials on farming, white drawing paper, crayons or markers
- Activity #7:   1 sheet of light-colored construction paper, crayons or markers, reference materials on farming

- Activity #8:   shoebox, glue, scissors, craft supplies
- Activity #9:   reference materials on mice and rats, 1 sheet of 12" x 18" light-colored construction paper, crayons or markers
- Activity #10: copy of page 37
- Activity #11: reference materials on using animals for scientific and medical research
- Activity #12: reference materials on medicinal plants, copy of page 38

Mrs. Frisby and the Rats of NIMH
Independent Contract

Name:_____ Number of activities to be completed: _____

1. Social Studies

Two themes that run through this book are friendship and kindness. For example, the shrew proves her friendship when she won't let the rats move the Frisby home without Mrs. Frisby being there, and Mr. Ages shows kindness when he gives Mrs. Frisby medicine for Timothy's pneumonia. Choose one incidence of friendship or kindness from the story. Then make sock puppets of the characters and act out the scene for your class. Ask your classmates to identify the act of friendship or kindness.

2. Writing

Mrs. Frisby has to suddenly move her family to avoid the danger of the plow. Think about what having to move suddenly would be like. What are some of the things that you would have to consider if you had to move? Write a story about your family or another family that has to move suddenly. Include problems that might occur when faced with a sudden move and details about how the members of the family might feel about moving.

3. Science

Several animals and their habitats are mentioned in *Mrs. Frisby and the Rats of NIMH,* including an owl in a tree, mice in a garden, a shrew in a garden, and of course, rats in their tunnels. Select one animal and research its natural habitat. Next, sketch the animal in its natural habitat. Then list several ways the animal has adapted to its habitat, including methods of camouflage and other protective devices. Finally, write a paragraph comparing the habitat in the novel to the animal's actual habitat.

4. Social Studies

Trust is an important value in this book. Do you think trust is important? Why or why not? Write a speech giving your opinions on trust. Recite your speech to the class. Then take a poll to find out how many of your classmates agree or disagree with your opinions and why.

5. Language Arts

Think about the different characters in the book. Which ones caused you to feel strong emotions? Obtain a copy of page 36 from your teacher and organize your thoughts about two characters that caused you to feel strong emotions.

6. Research

Mrs. Frisby's house is in a farmer's field that will be plowed soon. There are many tasks on a farm that are closely related to the seasons. Research farming, listing the tasks by the season in which they are performed. For example, crops are planted in the spring and fall. Create a farming guide by folding a sheet of paper into fourths accordion-style. On the front, design a cover with a title and farm-related art. On each of the inside folds, write the name of a season at the top and list each task on the appropriate fold. Add illustrations for each season.

Mrs. Frisby and the Rats of NIMH

Independent Contract

Name:_____ Number of activities to be completed: _____

 7. **Social Studies**

The Frisbys live on a farm. Farms have changed a lot in the past 150 years. Research farms and farm equipment to find out what has changed and when these changes have occurred. Then create a timeline with at least ten dates and changes in farming. Illustrate each one.

 8. **Art**

In chapter 1, the Frisbys' house is described as a "cinder block, the hollow kind with two oval holes through it." The house is lined with "leaves, grass, cloth, cotton fluff, feathers, and other soft things." Using a shoebox, create a diorama of the house. Divide the box into two parts. Use the book's description to help you make the inside. Include the tunnel that provides access to the house. Cover the outside of the box so that it resembles a cinder or concrete block.

 9. **Science**

The main characters in this book are mice and rats. Research mice and rats. Then draw a large mouse shape, a large cheese shape, and a large rat shape. In the mouse shape, list the characteristics unique to mice. In the rat shape, list the characteristics unique to rats. On the cheese shape, list the characteristics they have in common.

 10. **Math**

Although Mrs. Frisby doesn't have to pay to move her house, moving from one location to another in real life can be expensive. Obtain a copy of page 37 from your teacher and learn more about moving costs.

 11. **Research**

The rats in the book had been used by scientists for research. Do you think it is okay to use animals for medical and scientific research? Should there be limitations if animals are used? Research animal testing. List three reasons supporting the use of animals in research and three reasons opposing the use of animals. Write two editorial articles, one from each viewpoint. Share the articles with your class, and take a vote to find out whether most of your classmates are for or against using animals for scientific research.

 12. **Science**

When Mrs. Frisby goes to see Mr. Ages in chapter 2, he gives her some medicine for Timothy. The medicine is made from a plant. Plants have been used to make medicine for thousands of years. For example, in the past, people used the bark of a willow tree to help ease pain and reduce fever. People still use plants to make medicines. Obtain a copy of page 38 from your teacher and learn more about medicinal plants.

Mrs. Frisby and the Rats of NIMH

Strong Emotions!

Characters' actions in books can cause you to feel strong emotions. Think about two characters in *Mrs. Frisby and the Rats of NIMH* that made you feel strong emotions. Complete the first organizer below with information about a character that caused you to feel a strong positive emotion, such as happiness. Then complete the second organizer with information about a character that caused you to feel a strong negative emotion, such as anger.

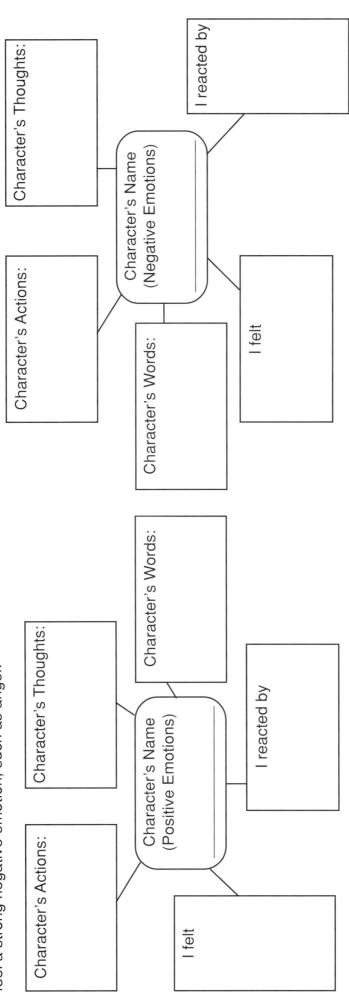

How are the actions of the first character you chose important to the story? _____

How are the actions of the second character you chose important to the story? _____

Do you think the book would be as good as it is if the actions of some of the characters didn't cause you to feel negative emotions? Why or why not? _____

Note to the teacher: Use with activity #5 on page 34.

Movin', Movin', Movin'

How much does it cost to move? That depends on the movers you hire. If you want them to pack your boxes and furniture into the truck, drive the truck to your new house, and move all your belongings in, it costs about $4.00 a mile. If you moved 2,000 miles at $4.00 a mile, the cost would be about $8,000.00.

Directions: Read each question below. Draw the map scale on an index card to find the distance between the cities listed. Then calculate the cost of the move by multiplying the distance by $4.00.

1. You have decided to move to the West from Augusta, Maine. If you move to Cheyenne, Wyoming, about how much will it cost? _____

2. You live in the Southwest, but want to move east. About how much will it cost to move from Phoenix, Arizona, to Birmingham, Alabama? _____

3. You have decided it is too cold in Fargo, North Dakota, and you want to move to Miami, Florida. About how much will it cost? _____

4. You are worried about earthquakes in San Francisco, California, and have decided to move to Nashville, Tennessee. About how much will it cost? _____

5. You have decided that you no longer want to live on the coast. You want to move from Houston, Texas, to Great Falls, Montana. About how much will it cost? _____

6. If you could move from your town to one of the cities on the map above, where would you move? About how much would it cost? _____

©2001 The Education Center, Inc. • *Contracts for Independent Readers • Fantasy* • TEC791 • Key p. 63

The Healing Power of Plants

Many plants are used to make medicines. Use reference materials to discover what ailments each plant listed below is used to relieve or treat. Then write the ailment on the corresponding leaf. The first one has been done for you.

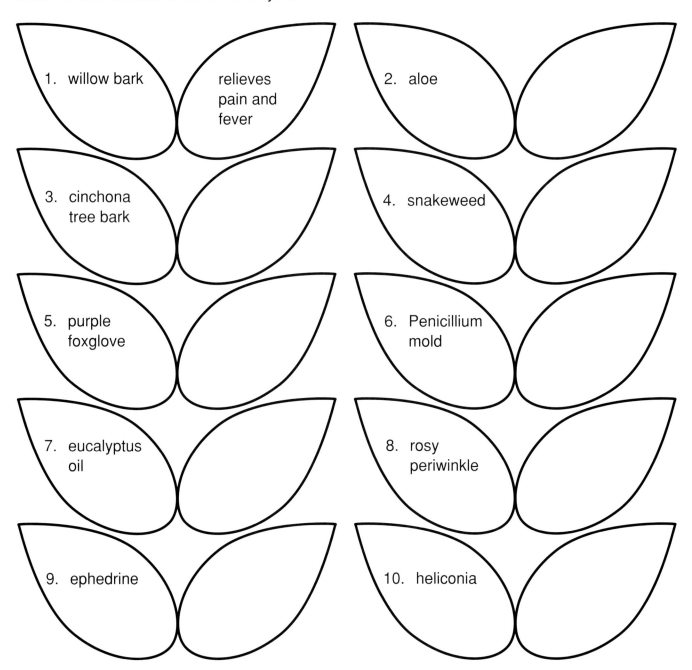

1. willow bark — relieves pain and fever

2. aloe

3. cinchona tree bark

4. snakeweed

5. purple foxglove

6. Penicillium mold

7. eucalyptus oil

8. rosy periwinkle

9. ephedrine

10. heliconia

Think about a disease that you have heard about on the news or read about in a textbook. Research to find out how it is treated and whether the treatment comes from plants. Write the name of the disease below and the information you discovered about its treatment. _____

_____

_____

_____

The Phantom Tollbooth
by Norton Juster

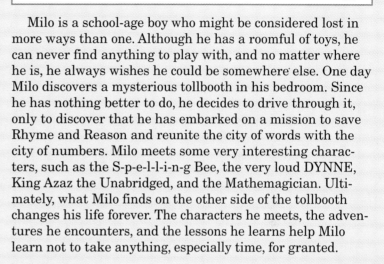

About the Book

Milo is a school-age boy who might be considered lost in more ways than one. Although he has a roomful of toys, he can never find anything to play with, and no matter where he is, he always wishes he could be somewhere else. One day Milo discovers a mysterious tollbooth in his bedroom. Since he has nothing better to do, he decides to drive through it, only to discover that he has embarked on a mission to save Rhyme and Reason and reunite the city of words with the city of numbers. Milo meets some very interesting characters, such as the S-p-e-l-l-i-n-g Bee, the very loud DYNNE, King Azaz the Unabridged, and the Mathemagician. Ultimately, what Milo finds on the other side of the tollbooth changes his life forever. The characters he meets, the adventures he encounters, and the lessons he learns help Milo learn not to take anything, especially time, for granted.

About the Author

Norton Juster seems to have a special affinity for writing books that play on words and numbers, such as *The Phantom Tollbooth*. Juster has fun with language and math in several other highly acclaimed children's books: *The Dot and the Line: A Romance in Lower Mathematics, Otter Nonsense,* and *As: A Surfeit of Similes.* Juster has also been an architect and a college professor.

Norton Juster was born on June 2, 1929, in New York, New York. He attended the University of Pennsylvania and the University of Liverpool. His interests include reading, bicycling, gardening, and cooking. He still occasionally makes public appearances and does book signings, even though his best-known book, *The Phantom Tollbooth*, was written in 1961.

Student Contract Materials List

- Activity #1: cardboard box; crayons, markers, or painting supplies
- Activity #2: paper, pencil
- Activity #3: paper, pencil
- Activity #4: blank cassette tape, tape recorder
- Activity #5: shoebox, arts-and-crafts supplies, twenty 3" x 5" index cards
- Activity #6: copy of page 42
- Activity #7: paper, pencil
- Activity #8: blank cassette tape, tape recorder
- Activity #9: reference materials on sound, household items
- Activity #10: light-colored construction paper, crayons or markers
- Activity #11: half sheet of poster board, crayons or markers
- Activity #12: copy of page 43

The Phantom Tollbooth

Independent Contract

Name:_____ Number of activities to be completed: _____

1. Art

In chapter 1, Milo receives a tollbooth. Make your own miniature version of the tollbooth using a cardboard box. On the top of the tollbooth, write the author's name and title of the book. On one of its sides, draw and label pictures of some of the characters Milo meets. On the opposite side, draw and label pictures of some of the places he visits. Then, on the back of the tollbooth, list some of the lessons that Milo learns throughout the story. Finally, decorate the front of the tollbooth as you imagine it to look.

2. Science

In chapter 10, Milo meets Chroma the Great, who believes that without color the world would be a really dull place. How much does color affect the way people feel and think? Conduct a survey to find out by asking at least 15 people the following questions: What is your favorite color? Least favorite? What color do you associate with being happy? Sad? Warm? Cold? When your data is collected, look for common answers that might indicate a majority feeling about a certain color. Then share the results with your class.

3. Math

Milo shops for words at the word market but realizes he doesn't have enough money to purchase them. Imagine that each letter of the alphabet is worth $.02 more than the letter before it. Start with A being worth $.02, B worth $.04, C worth $.06, and so on. Calculate the cost of the three words Milo picks *(quagmire, flabbergast, and upholstery).* Finally, make a list of interesting words from the book (at least one per chapter). Calculate the worth of each word.

4. Language Arts

Imagine that you are a reporter who has been assigned to interview one of the characters from *The Phantom Tollbooth.* Use the five Ws *(who, what, when, where,* and *why)* to help you write at least five interview questions. Then write the answer to each question as if you were that character. Make a tape recording of your interview. Record an introduction, followed by each question and its answer. Practice changing the sound of your voice so that the character and the reporter have different voices.

5. Writing

In chapter 8, King Azaz gives Milo a special box containing all the words he knows. King Azaz believes that with these words, there is no obstacle Milo cannot overcome. Make your own special box containing words that you would never want to do without. Decorate the outside of a shoebox to serve as your special word box. Then carefully select twenty words and write each word on the front of an index card. On the back of each card, explain why you chose that word.

6. Critical Thinking

During Milo's quest to rescue Rhyme and Reason, he receives several presents from people he meets along the way, each one having its own special purpose for the journey. Obtain a copy of page 42 from your teacher and complete it as directed.

The Phantom Tollbooth

Independent Contract

Name:_____ Number of activities to be completed: _____

7. Math

Tock's job is to make sure no one is wasting time. How do you spend your time? Create a chart to find out. Draw five columns and label each column as follows: Activity, Estimated Time Spent, Start Time, End Time, Actual Time Spent. In the first column, list your activities for one day. In the second column, write the amount of time that you think you spend doing each activity. Then, as you perform each activity, track and record your starting and ending times. Calculate the actual time you spend in column five. How close were your estimates?

8. Music

In chapter 10, Milo conducts a symphony of color. Conduct your own musical masterpiece by using the melody to "Twinkle, Twinkle Little Star" or another familiar tune. Replace the lyrics with words describing how the world contains all of the colors of the rainbow. When you are satisfied with your work, record your tune and then play it for the class.

9. Science

When Milo encounters Dr. Dischord and the awful DYNNE, he learns a lesson or two about sound. Research how sound is made. Then make several instruments using items you find around your house. Play the instruments to make different sounds—good and bad. Then give a sound demonstration to your class, sharing the different sounds that come from the instruments.

10. Language Arts

The meals that Milo eats during his journey are far from ordinary. He is offered dishes such as a square meal, a half-baked idea, and subtraction stew. Milo soon learns that not only their names are interesting but each dish also has its own unique properties. For example, no matter how much subtraction stew you eat, when you're finished, you're hungrier than when you started. Create your own menu, including at least ten different items with names that are a play on numbers or words, along with a description and illustration of each.

11. Language Arts

As Milo nears the Castle in the Air, he encounters demons that attempt to keep him from rescuing Rhyme and Reason. Imagine that there are demons that keep you from getting your work done. Perhaps there is a demon that keeps you from cleaning your room or waking up for school on time. Create a demon that is the cause of one of your problems. Then design a poster showing what your demon looks like. Also tell how your demon keeps you from doing your work and how you will defeat your demon.

12. Math

Milo's trip through the tollbooth takes him to so many new and exciting places that they become hard to keep track of. Obtain a copy of page 43 from your teacher to help you remember his journey.

Positively Perfect Presents

During Milo's quest to rescue Rhyme and Reason, he receives several presents. Each present has a special purpose for the journey. In the top portion of the suitcase below, draw a picture of the present each character gives to Milo. In the spaces provided, explain the purpose of each present. Include the page number from the book where you found the information. Then, in the bottom portion of the suitcase, name and draw four presents you would want to receive if you were the one traveling with Tock. In the spaces provided, explain why you chose each item.

Presents for Milo

1. King Azaz

2. Alec Bings

3. The Soundkeeper

4. The Mathemagician

Presents for Me

5. _____

6. _____

7. _____

8. _____

Note to the teacher: Use with activity #6 on page 40.

Graphing Milo's Journey

Milo's trip through the tollbooth takes him to many exciting places. Follow the directions below to plot on the coordinate graph each of his stops and the places he hears about.

Directions: Starting at the beginning of the list, plot each of the locations based on its *ordered pair*, or the numbers that name the point of intersection, shown in parentheses. After plotting each point, write its corresponding letter. Then connect it with a straight line to the previously plotted point. When you are finished, you will discover the character that helped Milo the most. The first two points have been done for you. **Hint:** To plot each point, go over and then up.

A. Milo's school (4,19)
B. Milo's room (4,17)
C. The tollbooth (6,17)
D. Expectations (5,22)
E. The Doldrums (0,18)
F. Foothills of Confusion (0,16)
G. Gate to the Word Market (3,14)
H. Dictionopolis (4,11)
I. The dungeon (1,3)
J. Kingdom of Wisdom (4,3)
K. Null (6,11)
L. Sea of Knowledge (5,3)
M. The scenic route (7,3)
N. Point of View (8,8)
O. Reality (14,6)
P. Illusions (12,1)
Q. Forest of Sight (15,1)
R. Forest's edge (17,6)
S. Valley of Sound (16,1)
T. Soundkeeper's fortress (18,1)
U. Island of Conclusions (21,9)
V. Digitopolis (19,14)
W. Infinity (13,20)
X. Mountains of Ignorance (9,22)
Y. Castle in the Air (5,22)

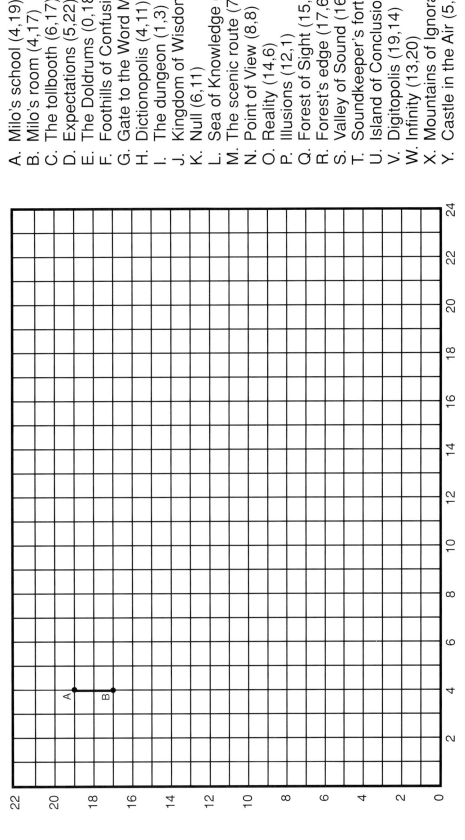

Who helped Milo the most? _____

©2001 The Education Center, Inc. • *Contracts for Independent Readers • Fantasy* • TEC791 • Key p. 64

Note to the teacher: Use with activity #12 on page 41.

Redwall
by Brian Jacques

About the Book

For as long as anyone can remember, the mice at Redwall Abbey in the Mossflower Wood have peacefully served others, healing the sick and aiding the poor. As the Abbey celebrates the Abbot's 50th anniversary, things are about to change. The mice, squirrels, moles, and others who call Mossflower home are under attack by Cluny the Scourge. Matthias, a young and timid mouse, must find the legendary sword of Martin the Warrior in order to save the Abbey. Using wit, courage, and teamwork, Matthias and the Redwall residents thwart Cluny's formidable forces.

About the Author

Brian Jacques was born in Liverpool, England, in 1939. As a child, Brian showed a talent for writing and a love of reading. Upon leaving school at the age of 15, he became a merchant seaman and traveled to many countries. The people he met and the things he saw became part of his later stories.

When Jacques returned to Liverpool, he worked as a police officer, a truck driver, and at several other vocations. Jacques first began writing professionally as a playwright. After meeting students at a school for the blind, he wrote *Redwall,* filling it with vivid scenes and characters to stir each child's imagination. *Redwall,* the winner of the Lancashire County Libraries Children's Book of the Year Award in 1988, is the first in a series of successful books about the fantasy land called Mossflower.

Student Contract Materials List

- Activity #1: paper, pencil
- Activity #2: square piece of muslin or other woven fabric, wire hanger, markers, stapler
- Activity #3: 12" x 18" sheet of white construction paper, colored pencils or markers
- Activity #4: graph paper, colored pencils, tape
- Activity #5: copy of page 47, dictionary
- Activity #6: poster board, reference materials on animals, crayons or markers
- Activity #7: three 9" x 12" sheets of white paper, three 8" lengths of blue ribbon
- Activity #8: reference materials on medieval castles, 12" x 18" sheet of construction paper, crayons or markers
- Activity #9: copy of page 48, colored pencils, highlighter
- Activity #10: 5 index cards
- Activity #11: copy of page 49, thesaurus
- Activity #12: 1 sheet of stationery, pens, markers

Redwall

Independent Contract

Name: _____ Number of activities to be completed: _____

 **Writing**

Long ago, Martin the Warrior saved Redwall, becoming a hero. Matthias learns what it means to be a hero as he tries to defeat Cluny the Scourge and his forces. Write a want ad for a hero describing the necessary skills and characteristics. Will your hero need courage, humility, good looks, or knowledge of military strategies? Include details in your want ad such as where to apply for the job, working conditions, and the salary or benefits being offered.

 Art

The ancient, beautiful tapestry hanging in Redwall's Great Hall portrays Martin the Warrior. Create a new Redwall tapestry that features Matthias as the hero. On muslin, use a pencil to sketch the details of the brave mouse's quest for the sword of Martin the Warrior. Include illustrations of the main characters and the battles fought against Cluny. Add rich, beautiful colors to the tapestry. Staple your work of art to a wire hanger and proudly display it.

 Social Studies

At the front of the book is a simple map of Mossflower Wood and Redwall Abbey. Re-create the map in more detail. Label the main parts of the Abbey and the important battle sites. Show the locations of the clues that Matthias follows to find Martin's sword. Include a legend and a compass rose on your map. Then add a colorful, decorative border showing characters or items from the story.

 Math

Many animals play key roles in *Redwall*. Look back through chapters 2, 3, and 18 in Book 1 and chapter 5 in Book 3 to find the different animals mentioned. List each animal by its name and species. Then sort the list into groups, such as rats, mice, and voles. Count the animals in each group and record the data. Create a graph to present your data. Color-code the graph to indicate which animals belong to the Redwall forces and which belong to Cluny's forces. Be sure to add a key! Then write a paragraph summarizing the data and tape it to the back of your graph.

 Language Arts

Brother Methuselah and Matthias work together to unravel the riddle that tells the original location of Martin the Warrior's sword. Decipher the meaning of some of the challenging words in *Redwall* by using a dictionary to discover their meanings. Obtain a copy of page 47 from your teacher and complete it as directed.

 Science

Many types of small animals populate the Redwall story. Select four animals from the list below. Use reference materials to learn about each animal's habitat, physical characteristics, diet, and habits. Write a short paragraph about each one based on what you learn. Then divide a sheet of poster board into four sections. Label each section with the name of one animal. Draw a picture of the animal and copy your descriptive paragraph under its illustration.

| mouse | otter | weasel | fox | hedgehog |
| stoat | vole | badger | rat | ferret |

Redwall

Independent Contract

Name:_____ Number of activities to be completed: _____

(7.) Critical Thinking

In Book 1, chapter 1, Matthias learns the guiding vows of Redwall Abbey. Later, in Book 1, chapter 8, Redtooth recites Cluny's articles of war to the newly recruited rats, ferrets, and weasels. Write the vows and articles, each on a separate sheet of paper in fancy, old-fashioned writing. Add a title and decorations to make the writing appear official and important. Then list four guiding principles you would like to follow in your own life. Copy them on a third sheet. Roll each document to form a scroll. Tie each scroll with ribbon.

(8.) Research

Redwall Abbey is built much like a medieval castle. Use reference materials to learn how castles were defended in the Middle Ages. Based on this information, choose three defense structures that could be added to better protect Redwall. Would you add a moat, extra towers, or a drawbridge? Draw the Abbey in as much detail as possible. Add sketches of the new defense structures you choose. Label each defense structure and write an explanation of its use. Then color your new design of Redwall Abbey.

(9.) Reading

In literature, *conflict* is the problem that characters face in a story. One of the main conflicts in *Redwall* is between Matthias and Cluny. Look back through the book and reread sections that describe these two leaders. Think about how they are similar and different. Then obtain a copy of page 48 from your teacher and complete it according to the directions.

(10.) Writing

In Book 2, chapter 4, Matthias and Brother Methuselah puzzle over the meaning of the clues in an ancient poem. They solve the riddle and find the next clue to the location of Martin's sword. Write riddles about five different objects in your classroom. In each riddle, give clues about the color, location, function or purpose, and other relevant details of the object. Print each riddle on the front of an index card. Write its answer on the back of the card. Challenge classmates to solve your riddles.

(11.) Language Arts

Brian Jacques vividly conveys the action of the story by using powerful, accurate verbs that spark the reader's imagination. Begin a quest to find the meanings of verbs that help the reader see the action. Obtain a copy of page 49 from your teacher and complete it according to the directions. Your search will help you build word power to make your own writing more colorful and exciting.

(12.) Critical Thinking

As they celebrate Father Abbot's 50th anniversary, the residents savor many delicious foods and drinks. On your paper, make five columns labeled "drinks," "appetizers," "main dishes," "side dishes," and "desserts." Reread Book 1, chapter 3, and list each food mentioned under the column heading that best describes it. Next, invent six new dishes and two new drinks using any fruits, vegetables, nuts, and fish that might be found in the area of Mossflower Wood. Then create a menu using a sheet of stationery and fancy writing. Include descriptions and illustrations of these mouthwatering dishes.

Mystery of Martin's Sword

To recover the sword, Matthias has to decipher challenging clues. Use your powers of deduction and a dictionary to discover where Matthias finds the sword of Martin the Warrior.

Directions: Read each definition below. Then record the word from the word list it defines in the blanks provided.

1. device that shows the way the wind is blowing
    _____ _____ _____ _____ _____ _____ _____   _____ _____ ⦿ _____

2. place where stone is cut or blasted out
    _____ ⦿ _____ _____ _____ _____

3. hinged or sliding door in a floor, ceiling, or roof
    ⦿ _____ _____ _____   _____ _____ _____ _____

4. title of respect for a large rural landowner
    _____ _____ ⦿ _____ _____ _____

5. venomous snake
    _____ ⦿ _____ _____ _____

6. document written by hand
    ⦿ _____ _____ _____ _____ _____ _____ _____ _____

7. type of small finch
    ⦿ _____ _____ _____ _____ _____

8. sheath for the blade of a sword
    _____ _____ _____ _____ ⦿ _____ _____ _____

9. heavy woven cloth with decorative design
    _____ ⦿ _____ _____ _____ _____ _____ _____

10. long hall or passageway
    _____ ⦿ _____ _____ _____ _____ _____

11. statue or other image
    _____ ⦿ _____ _____ _____ _____

12. piece of wood or stone set under a door
    _____ ⦿ _____ _____ _____ _____ _____ _____ _____

Word List

quarry

tapestry

scabbard

effigy

manuscript

trap door

sparrow

squire

corridor

threshold

viper

weather vane

Directions: Fill in the letter from each shield above on the line with the corresponding definition number below to show where Matthias finds the sword of Martin the Warrior.

_____ _____ _____ _____ _____ _____ _____ _____   _____ _____ _____ _____ _____ _____ _____ _____ _____ _____ _____ _____ '   _____ _____ _____
9   7   6   10   8   11   2   7   5   10   4   7   10   1   3   11   11   3   12   7   8   11   1

©2001 The Education Center, Inc. • *Contracts for Independent Readers* • Fantasy • TEC791 • Key p. 64

Note to the teacher: Use with activity #5 on page 45.

Character and Conflict

Directions: Use colored pencils to draw and color portraits of Matthias and Cluny the Scourge in the ovals below. On the lines next to each portrait, write a brief summary of each character's personality traits. Highlight any traits that Matthias and Cluny have in common. Then, below the portraits, describe a time when Matthias and Cluny are in direct conflict. Tell who triumphs in the struggle and how he defeats the other.

Personality Traits	Matthias	C o n f l i c t	Cluny the Scourge	Personality Traits

Describe a conflict. What happened? _____

Who triumphs? How? _____

Note to the teacher: Use with activity #9 on page 46.

Name

Quest for Verbs

Part I Directions: Read each sentence below and think about the underlined verb's meaning. Find each verb in a thesaurus. Choose a powerful synonym to replace the underlined verb. Copy the sentence with the new verb in the space provided.

Example: Matthias <u>walked</u> quietly out of the Abbey.
Matthias <u>sneaked</u> quietly out of the Abbey.

1. The cat <u>poked</u> Matthias with his paw.

   _____

2. One of the shrews <u>took</u> the stone.

   _____

3. Matthias <u>lifted</u> the bundle of food over his shoulder.

   _____

4. "Will you lot shut up!" <u>said</u> the shrew, looking back at his comrades.

   _____

5. Captain Snow <u>said</u> that he would never eat another mouse or shrew if Matthias killed Asmodeus.

   _____

6. Matthias <u>fell</u> into the mouth of a marmalade cat.

   _____

7. Matthias <u>moved</u> along the path in the woods.

   _____

8. Matthias <u>threw</u> the stone into the river and set off by himself in search of the snake.

   _____

9. The screech of the owl <u>broke</u> the silence.

   _____

10. The cat <u>looked</u> at Matthias in disgust.

Part II Directions: Look back through *Redwall* to find ten powerful verbs. Then write them in the bricks below to complete the *Redwall* word wall.

Redwall Word Wall

Note to the teacher: Use with activity #11 on page 46.

Tuck Everlasting
by Natalie Babbitt

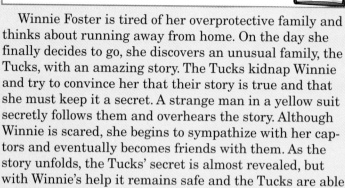

About the Book

Winnie Foster is tired of her overprotective family and thinks about running away from home. On the day she finally decides to go, she discovers an unusual family, the Tucks, with an amazing story. The Tucks kidnap Winnie and try to convince her that their story is true and that she must keep it a secret. A strange man in a yellow suit secretly follows them and overhears the story. Although Winnie is scared, she begins to sympathize with her captors and eventually becomes friends with them. As the story unfolds, the Tucks' secret is almost revealed, but with Winnie's help it remains safe and the Tucks are able to escape.

About the Author

Natalie Babbitt was born in Ohio on July 28, 1932, during the Great Depression. Her family moved around the state a lot, so Natalie and her sister had to adjust to new neighborhoods and new schools quite often. Natalie's family stuck together through it all. Her mother constantly encouraged and supported her desire to become an illustrator of children's books. Natalie has described herself as a skinny kid who loved toasted-cheese sandwiches and anything chocolate. She hated stories that tried to teach her things. Her favorite book was *Alice in Wonderland*.

Babbitt married her husband, Samuel, after graduating from Smith College, where she majored in art. The two collaborated on their first book, with Natalie illustrating and Samuel writing. Once her husband became too busy with his job to write stories, Babbitt began writing and illustrating her own books for children. She says that she is now able to express herself much better with words than she ever could with just pictures. Babbitt has three children—two boys and a girl—as well as a dog and three cats.

Student Contract Materials List

- Activity #1: paper, pencil
- Activity #2: copy of page 53, 20 small paper cups, tap water, bottled spring water, permanent marker
- Activity #3: reference materials on nomadic Native Americans, 1 sheet of 12" x 18" light-colored construction paper
- Activity #4: paper, pencil
- Activity #5: crayons, colored pencils, markers, or painting supplies; white paper
- Activity #6: paper, pencil
- Activity #7: reference materials on the benefits of drinking water, white paper, crayons or markers
- Activity #8: copy of page 54
- Activity #9: blank tape, tape recorder
- Activity #10: paper, pencil
- Activity #11: copy of page 55, 2 sheets of white paper, crayons or markers
- Activity #12: shoebox, arts-and-crafts supplies, glue, 1 index card

Tuck Everlasting
Independent Contract

Name:_____ Number of activities to be completed: _____

 ### 1. Language Arts

Think about the toad that Winnie pours the spring water over at the end of chapter 25. He is later seen by Tuck, who almost runs him over. What do you think a toad that could live forever would do all day—forever? Write a story about the toad that lived forever. Describe his day-to-day activities and how the world around him keeps changing.

 ### 2. Science

In *Tuck Everlasting* a sip of spring water will give you immortality. Spring water can also quench your thirst on a hot summer day, but does it really taste better than tap water? Obtain a copy of page 53 from your teacher and find out if your friends and family think spring water tastes better than tap water.

 ### 3. Social Studies

To avoid being discovered, the Tucks never stay in one place for very long. The term *nomads* refers to groups of people who wander from place to place. Some Native American tribes were nomads, including the Plains Indians, the Papago, the Pima, and later the Sioux and the Cheyenne. Choose three nomadic tribes and then research them to find out how and why each tribe wandered from place to place. Then create a chart to show the differences between, and the similarities to, the Tucks' way of life and that of the nomadic tribes.

 ### 4. Language Arts

When Winnie is captured by the Tucks and taken to their dusty old house, she is concerned about her safety. Suppose that she became so concerned that she devised a way to send a message to her family, using a secret code. Make up a secret code using symbols or numbers to represent the letters of the alphabet. Then write a secret message from Winnie, asking for help. Write the decoded message on a separate sheet of paper. Then give a friend the code and the secret message to see if he or she can solve it.

 ### 5. Art

Natalie Babbitt describes the woods near the Foster house very clearly, especially in chapters 1 and 5. Think about the author's words. Do they create a picture in your mind? Draw or paint a picture of how you see the wooded area from the way she describes it.

 ### 6. Language Arts

Pretend that you are a TV reporter who has found out the secret of the spring and that you know Winnie is being held captive inside the Tucks' house. Write what you would say in a newscast while standing outside the Tucks' house when the man in the yellow suit appears, and then when the constable appears. Share your newscast with the class.

Tuck Everlasting
Independent Contract

Name:_____ Number of activities to be completed: _____

7. Science

All living things need water to survive, but can it help you live longer? Nutritionists recommend drinking about eight glasses of water a day for healthful living. Research the health benefits of water. Then create a pamphlet advertising the benefits of water and encouraging students to drink more.

8. Science

Unlike the Tucks, most human beings live for about 70 years. Which animals live longer than humans? Which animals don't live as long? Obtain a copy of page 54 from your teacher and find out how long some animals' life spans are.

9. Music

Think about one of your favorite songs. Come up with new lyrics to go with the tune, changing the words to fit the plot of *Tuck Everlasting*. For example, the beginning of the *Brady Bunch* theme song could be changed to "Here's the story of a girl named Winnie, who was sick and tired of living with her folks." Make a tape recording of your song and then play it for your class.

10. Critical Thinking

The Tucks have the power to live forever. Would you want to live forever? List reasons for and against living forever. Then write an essay explaining whether you would want to live forever. If you would want to live forever, include your opinion of the best age to remain.

11. Language Arts

Natalie Babbitt, the author of *Tuck Everlasting,* uses a lot of metaphors and similes to describe things in the book. Look up the definitions of *metaphor* and *simile.* Then obtain a copy of page 55 from your teacher and discover the ways in which Babbitt uses these two devices to paint pictures for her readers.

12. Social Studies

Imagine how things would have been different if Winnie had decided to stay with the Tucks. What do you think she would have done to make their house more like what she was used to? Reread the description of the Tucks' house in chapter 10. Then make a shoebox diorama with one half showing how the house looked before she moves in and the other half showing how it might look after she moves in. On an index card, explain the changes she might make and why she makes them. Glue the card to the top of the box.

Tap Water Taste Test

Which do you think tastes better—tap water or spring water? Find out whether there is really a difference by following the steps below to conduct your own taste test.

Question: Which tastes better, spring water or tap water?

Hypothesis: (how you think the majority of the people will answer the question) _____

_____

Materials: 20 small paper cups, tap water, bottled spring water, permanent marker

Procedure: 1. Use a marker to write "A" on ten of the cups and "B" on ten of the cups.
2. Fill the cups marked "A" halfway with tap water.
3. Fill the cups marked "B" halfway with spring water. (Do not tell anyone which is which.)
4. Ask at least ten people to taste both types of water. Ask each person which water he or she prefers. Make a check mark in the appropriate column.

Observations:

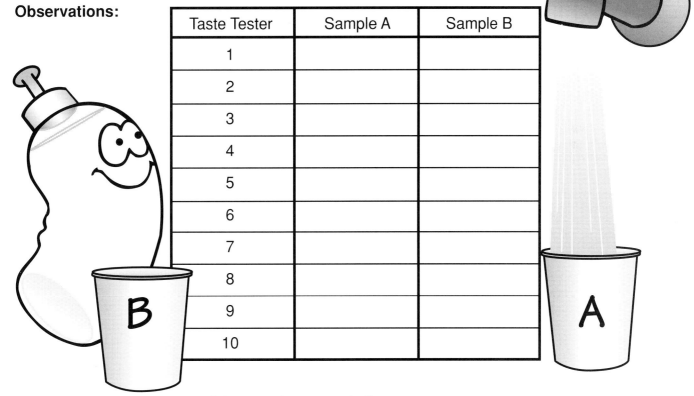

Taste Tester	Sample A	Sample B
1		
2		
3		
4		
5		
6		
7		
8		
9		
10		

Results: (how the majority of the people responded) _____

_____

Conclusion: (Was your hypothesis correct? Why or why not?) _____

_____

Live a Little or Live a Lot!

Most humans live for about 70 years. Imagine living forever! Forever is a long time. How long do other animals live? Follow the directions below to compare the life spans of a few of the many animals on earth.

Directions: Carefully read the chart below. Then answer the questions that follow.

Approximate Life Spans in Years

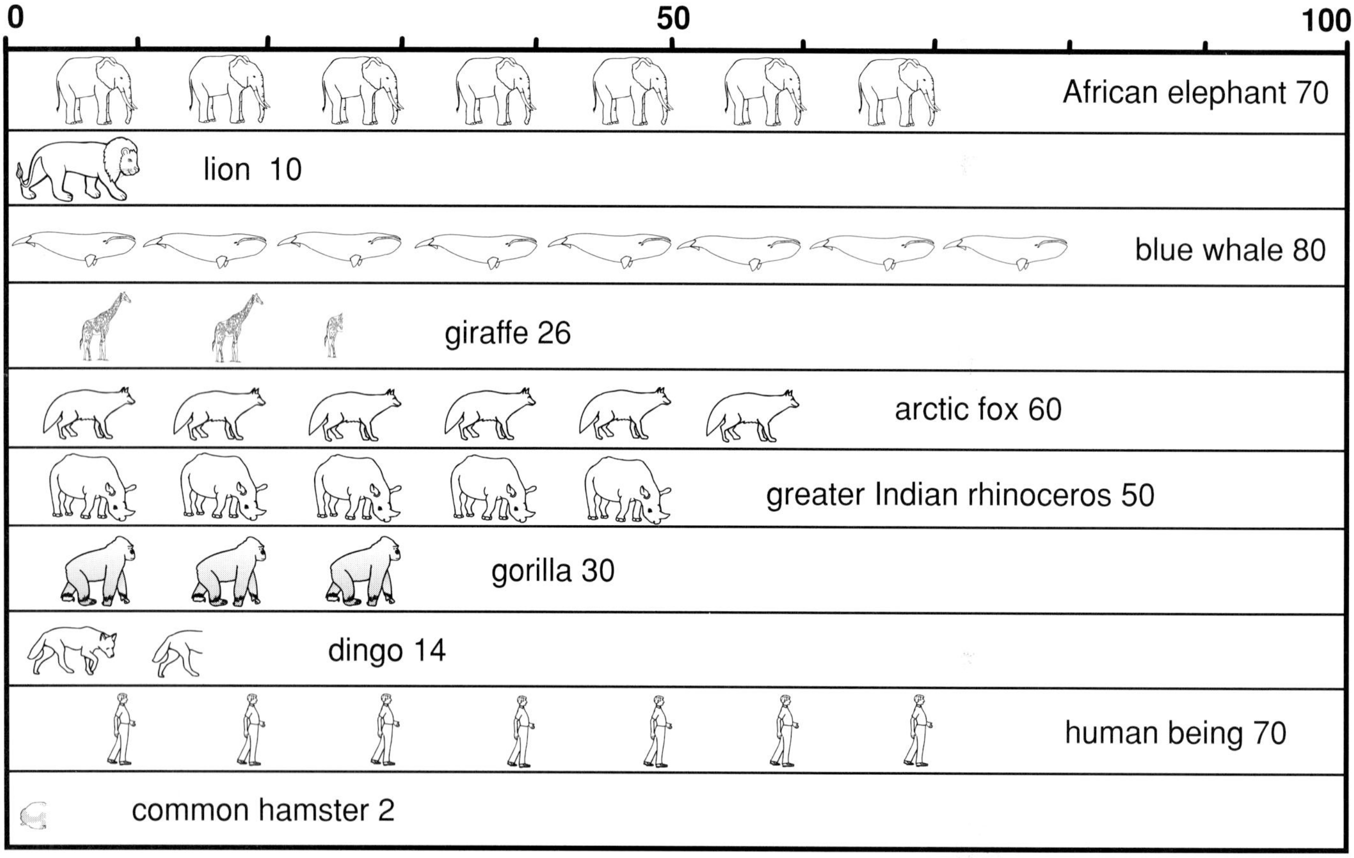

0
50
100
African elephant 70
lion 10
blue whale 80
giraffe 26
arctic fox 60
greater Indian rhinoceros 50
gorilla 30
dingo 14
human being 70
common hamster 2

1. Which animals live as long as humans or longer? ________________________
____
2. Which animals don't live as long as humans? ________________________
____
3. According to this chart, what animal lives the longest? ________________
4. How much longer does a blue whale live than a giraffe? ________________
5. How much longer does a gorilla live than a common hamster? ____________
6. Which five life spans can be combined to equal exactly 200? ____________
7. If a gorilla could triple its life span, how long would it live? If it could quadruple its life span?
____
8. How many times would a common hamster have to double its life span to equal the life span of a blue whale? ________________________
9. Why do you think the common hamster has such a short life span? ____________
____
10. Why do you think the blue whale has such a long life span? ______________
____

 Note to the teacher: Use with activity #8 on page 52.

As Pretty As a Picture

Natalie Babbitt uses metaphors and similes to help the reader "see" what she is describing. Follow the directions below to discover what each metaphor and simile helps you see!

Part I: Think about the _literal_, or exact, meaning of each item below. Then, on a separate sheet of paper, draw four picture frames. Inside each frame, draw the literal meaning of each item. The first one has been done for you.

1. chapter 6: "It was **like a ribbon tying her to familiar things.**"
2. chapter 9: "…it was as if they had **slipped in under a giant colander.**"
3. chapter 9: "…saw an expression there that made her feel **like an unexpected present, wrapped in pretty paper and tied with ribbons…**"
4. chapter 10: "An ancient green-plush sofa lolled alone in the center, **like yet another mossy fallen log…**"
5. chapter 11: "I got a feeling this whole thing is going to come apart **like wet bread.**"

Part II: Think about the _figurative_, or nonliteral, meaning of each item below. Then, on a separate sheet of paper, draw four picture frames. Inside each frame, draw the figurative meaning of each item. The first one has been done for you.

6. chapter 6: "…who would tumble her into a blanket and bear her off **like a sack of potatoes…**"
7. chapter 6: "…though her heart was pounding and **her backbone felt like a pipe full of cold running water…**"
8. chapter 8: "Jesse sang funny old songs in a loud voice and **swung like a monkey** from the branches of trees…"
9. chapter 9: "…**the graceful arms of the pines** stretched out protectively in every direction."
10. chapter 9: "But everything else was motionless, **dry as biscuit…**"

©2001 The Education Center, Inc. • _Contracts for Independent Readers • Fantasy_ • TEC791

Note to the teacher: Use with activity #11 on page 52.

A Wrinkle in Time

by Madeleine L'Engle

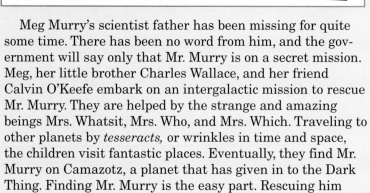

About the Book

Meg Murry's scientist father has been missing for quite some time. There has been no word from him, and the government will say only that Mr. Murry is on a secret mission. Meg, her little brother Charles Wallace, and her friend Calvin O'Keefe embark on an intergalactic mission to rescue Mr. Murry. They are helped by the strange and amazing beings Mrs. Whatsit, Mrs. Who, and Mrs. Which. Traveling to other planets by *tesseracts,* or wrinkles in time and space, the children visit fantastic places. Eventually, they find Mr. Murry on Camazotz, a planet that has given in to the Dark Thing. Finding Mr. Murry is the easy part. Rescuing him will take faith, courage, and, most of all, love.

About the Author

Madeleine L'Engle was born on November 29, 1918, in New York, New York. She lived there until she was 12, when she and her parents moved to Europe. Later, they returned to the United States, and Madeleine finished high school in South Carolina. She attended Smith College and then returned to New York City.

Madeleine began writing at the age of five. During her teenage years, writing stories, poems, and novels allowed her to escape from her problems into her imagination. Madeleine traveled extensively as a child and developed an appreciation for visiting other lands and seeing the differences in the ways people live around the world.

After college, L'Engle worked in theater. She attempted to publish in magazines and published her first novel, *The Small Rain,* in 1945. Since then, L'Engle has published many works. *A Wrinkle in Time* won the Newbery Medal in 1963. Other books by L'Engle include *A Ring of Endless Light* and *A Swiftly Tilting Planet.* She continues to live in New York, spending her time teaching, writing, and traveling.

Student Contract Materials List

- Activity #1: 10 student-selected novels
- Activity #2: ½ sheet of poster board, painting supplies, scissors, crayons or markers, glue, cotton balls
- Activity #3: paper, pencil
- Activity #4: copy of page 59
- Activity #5: calculator (optional)
- Activity #6: 9" x 12" sheet of light-colored construction paper, stapler

- Activity #7: white paper, crayons or markers
- Activity #8: 3 sheets of white paper, scissors, crayons or markers, stapler, several books of quotations
- Activity #9: 10 blank 3" x 5" index cards, crayons or markers
- Activity #10: copy of page 60
- Activity #11: reference materials on historical figures
- Activity #12: paper, pencil

A Wrinkle in Time

Independent Contract

Name:_____ Number of activities to be completed: _____

 1. Writing

Madeleine L'Engle's first sentence in *A Wrinkle in Time* is "It was a dark and stormy night." The sentence hints at the mood and introduces the story's setting. Select ten novels from the library. Copy the title, author, and first sentence of each novel, skipping several spaces between each entry. Think about each book's introductory sentence. Do you think the sentence is mostly about the book's plot, setting, character, or a combination of these? Write your answer in the space after each entry and tell why you chose that answer.

 2. Art

A Wrinkle in Time contains some very strange and unusual settings! Choose one of the places the children visit, such as Uriel, Ixchel, or Camazotz. Create a three-dimensional picture of the setting. First, paint a background, such as a sky or horizon, on poster board and cut it out. Next, draw and cut out a landscape or building skyline to represent the midground. Then draw and cut out a foreground, including characters. Glue cotton balls to the backs of the foreground and midground cutouts. Then line up the lower edges and glue the three layers of scenery together to create your three-dimensional setting.

 3. Writing

Reread the description of the strictly controlled life on Camazotz in chapter 6. Houses and flowers are all alike. Children jump rope and bounce balls in perfect rhythm. After watching the paperboy throw papers with perfect consistency, Calvin wonders if baseball is played on the strange planet. Think about a daily event or special activity in your life, such as eating lunch in the school cafeteria or visiting a beach, zoo, or park. Brainstorm ways the activity would be different for people on Camazotz. Then write a diary entry describing the activity as though you are a space explorer who is viewing it on Camazotz.

 4. Language Arts

Madeleine L'Engle uses very challenging vocabulary in *A Wrinkle in Time.* Obtain a copy of page 59 from your teacher and review the meanings of some of these words.

 5. Math

Meg and the others tesser through the universe because the distance between stars is immense. Vast distances in space are measured in *light-years*, or the distance light travels through space in one year (5,880,000,000,000 miles). Calculate the distance in miles from Earth to each star listed below by multiplying the number of light-years shown by 5,880,000,000,000 miles. Then rank the stars in order from the closest to the most distant.

Sirius: 8.6 light-years   Arcturus: 34 light-years
Vega: 25 light-years   Aldebaran: 60 light-years
Altair: 16 light-years

 6. Reading

Mrs. Whatsit grows wings when she metamorphoses. Make your own "Whatsit Wing" book summary. Accordion-fold a 9" x 12" sheet of construction paper, making each fold about one inch wide. On each of the 12 surfaces, write one chapter number and an important event from that chapter. When you have finished, staple one end so your summary resembles a wing.

A Wrinkle in Time

Independent Contract

Name:_____ Number of activities to be completed: _____

 7. **Art**

Aunt Beast has many tentacles, but no eyes. At first, Meg finds her strange and frightening. Later, Meg realizes that Aunt Beast "must have senses of which she could not even dream." Humans rely on their five senses. Other creatures may depend on different senses. Bats and dolphins use a kind of natural sonar called *echolocation.* Some snakes have heat-sensing organs for finding warm-blooded prey. Create your own alien species that uses a unique sense. Draw a picture of it. Then write an explanation of how it is specially adapted to receive information about its surroundings.

 8. **Language Arts**

Mrs. Who often recites famous quotations as a way to share important thoughts with the children. Study a book of quotations on different topics, such as honesty and friendship. Choose 11 quotations that you feel are meaningful to make your own "Mrs. Who's Little Instruction Booklet." Fold and then cut three sheets of paper to make 12 rectangles. Staple the rectangles along one edge to create a booklet. Make a cover by writing the title and your name on the top rectangle. On each booklet page, copy a quotation and the name of its author. Finally, illustrate the pages and the booklet cover.

 9. **Critical Thinking**

A Wrinkle in Time contains a wide variety of realistic and fantasy characters. Realistic characters look and behave in realistic or believable ways. Fantasy characters may look unusual and often accomplish their goals in mysterious or magical ways. Label five index cards "realistic" and five "fantasy" to create character trading cards. Choose five characters of each type from the book. On the top half of each card, write one character's name and draw a portrait of that character. Below the portrait, describe the traits that support your opinion that the character is realistic or fantastical.

 10. **Language Arts**

Throughout the book, Meg attempts to find her father. She takes many steps to achieve her goal, but she doesn't do it alone! A host of human and nonhuman characters helps her along the way. Obtain a copy of page 60 from your teacher and find out more about the characters who help Meg reach her goal.

 11. **Social Studies**

Mrs. Whatsit and the children name several historic figures who fought for Good against the Dark Thing. Imagine that your school is holding an election to select history's most outstanding "Fighter Against the Dark Thing." In your opinion, which historic figure most deserves the honor? Use reference materials to learn about the life of the person you select and the contributions he or she made. Then write a persuasive nomination speech in which you describe the person and how his or her contributions have made the world a better place to live. Practice your speech. Then share it with your class.

 12. **Writing**

Reread chapter 12 where Mrs. Whatsit compares human life to a sonnet. Following the pattern below carefully, write a sonnet about something that is important to you, such as a friend or belief.

1. Sonnets have three sets of four lines called *quatrains,* followed by a two-line set called a *couplet.*
2. The rhyming pattern is *abab, cdcd, efef, gg.* This means that, for each quatrain, the last words of the first and third lines rhyme, and the last words of the second and fourth lines rhyme. The last words of the couplet lines rhyme as well.

The Happy Medium's Crystal Ball

Directions: For each sentence below, use context clues in the book or use a dictionary to determine the meaning of the underlined word. Write the meaning of each word on the back of this sheet.

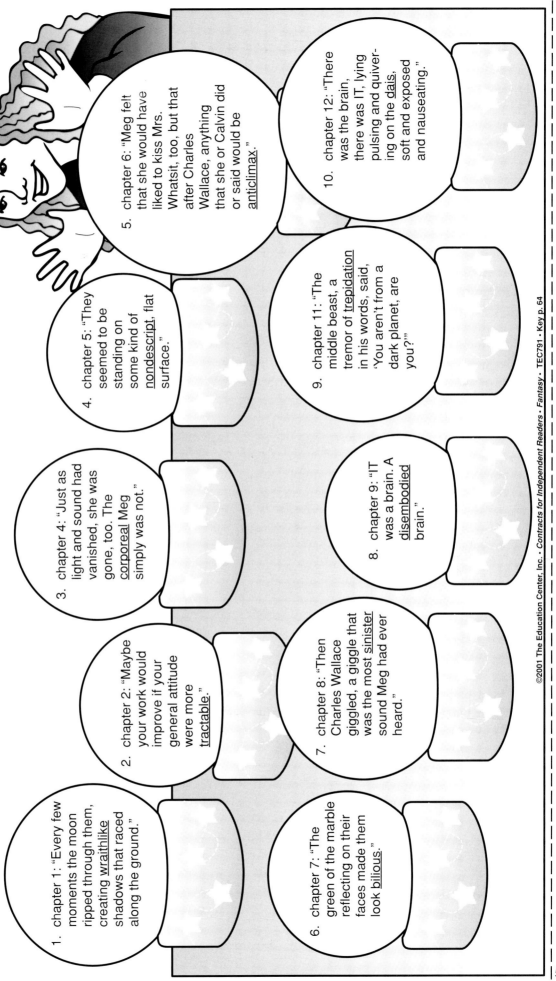

1. chapter 1: "Every few moments the moon ripped through them, creating <u>wraithlike</u> shadows that raced along the ground."

2. chapter 2: "Maybe your work would improve if your general attitude were more <u>tractable</u>."

3. chapter 4: "Just as light and sound had vanished, she was gone, too. The <u>corporeal</u> Meg simply was not."

4. chapter 5: "They seemed to be standing on some kind of <u>nondescript</u>, flat surface."

5. chapter 6: "Meg felt that she would have liked to kiss Mrs. Whatsit, too, but that after Charles Wallace, anything that she or Calvin did or said would be <u>anticlimax</u>."

6. chapter 7: "The green of the marble reflecting on their faces made them look <u>bilious</u>."

7. chapter 8: "Then Charles Wallace giggled, a giggle that was the most <u>sinister</u> sound Meg had ever heard."

8. chapter 9: "IT was a brain. A <u>disembodied</u> brain."

9. chapter 11: "The middle beast, a tremor of <u>trepidation</u> in his words, said, 'You aren't from a dark planet, are you?'"

10. chapter 12: "There was the brain, there was IT, lying pulsing and quivering on the <u>dais</u>, soft and exposed and nauseating."

Note to the teacher: Use with activity #4 on page 57.

I Get By With a Little Help From My Friends

Though faced with many challenges, Meg successfully completes her mission. Successful people set goals and work to achieve them. To increase their chances of success, they also accept help from people who care about them.

Directions: On the star, describe Meg's goal. Along the path, list at least four of the actions she takes to achieve her goal. Then, on each moon, tell how each person helps Meg along the way.

Mrs. Whatsit

Goal:

Mrs. Who

Mrs. Which

Happy Medium

Aunt Beast

Actions:

Meg

©2001 The Education Center, Inc. • *Contracts for Independent Readers* • *Fantasy* • TEC791 • Key p. 64

Note to the teacher: Use with activity #10 on page 58.

Fantasy Features to Ignite Your Imagination

Soar through space, travel through time, argue with animals, and manipulate magic with this collection of fantasy novels.

The 13th Floor: A Ghost Story by Sid Fleischman • What happens when you open the door onto a 13th floor that doesn't exist? Adventure on the high seas with ghosts, of course! Buddy Stebbins must find his way back to the present, but not before he finds his sister, helps his ancestors, and defends a young girl accused of witchcraft.

The Borrowers by Mary Norton • The Clock family live in a miniature world beneath the floorboards of a country house. They borrow everything they need from the "human beans" above. But once they are seen, they must escape before their world is discovered.

The Castle in the Attic by Elizabeth Winthrop • William has just received a model of a castle, complete with a drawbridge and a tiny knight. When the knight comes to life, William realizes that the only way to help him regain his kingdom is to become the size of the knight and enter the castle as a squire.

Charmed Life by Diana Wynne Jones • Cat and Gwendolen have just been invited to live in Chrestomanci Castle. Being the most talented young witch on Coven Street had meant something, but in the castle, Gwendolen isn't even allowed to use her powers.

The Cricket in Times Square by George Selden • Who would befriend a cricket? How about a mouse, a boy, and a cat? That's exactly who Chester Cricket meets when he arrives at the Bellinis' newsstand in the Times Square subway station. Now the friends must work together to save the almost-bankrupt newsstand.

Half Magic by Edward Eager • Jane, Mark, Katharine, and Martha are having a boring summer until Jane finds a coin that grants wishes. Well, almost. It grants half-wishes. A lot of trouble can come from wishes that only come halfway true.

Jeremy Thatcher, Dragon Hatcher by Bruce Coville • Jeremy loves animals. He keeps more than a dozen cages with mice, gerbils, hamsters, and guinea pigs. But what will he do with his dragon hatchling, especially when she starts watching his other pets with a hungry eye?

Running Out of Time by Margaret Peterson Haddix • Is it 1840 or 1996? That depends on whether you live in the reconstructed village of Clifton or the outside world. Jessie must leave the security of the village and venture into the unknown world to save the dying children of Clifton.

The Secret of Platform 13 by Eva Ibbotson • Once every nine years, a secret door opens to a magical island. Now four unlikely heroes—an ogre, a hag, a wizard, and a fey—must face the outer world to rescue their prince and return him to the island.

Shoebag by Mary James • Once a cockroach, always a cockroach. Or so Shoebag thought until the day he changed from an ordinary cockroach into a little boy. Now Shoebag must find a way to protect his family and get back the life he once knew.

Stinker From Space by Pamela F. Service • Tsynq Yr, pronounced Stinker, is from the Sylon Confederacy. While evading an enemy Zarnk cruiser, he is launched through space to Earth. On Earth he claims the body of a skunk and befriends Karen. Now the two of them must find a way to get Stinker back to his world.

The Wish Giver by Bill Brittain • For only $0.50 the Wish Giver will give you any wish you desire. But be careful what you wish for because you just might get it—exactly as you asked for it.

Answer Keys

Page 9
Part I:
2. $9
3. 7 KJs
4. $30
5. $12
6. 14½ KJs
7. $33
8. 3½ KJs
9. $18
10. $15
11. 17 KJs
12. $36
13. 4½ KJs
14. $3
15. $51
16. $6
17. 9½ KJs
18. $24
19. $39
20. $48
21. $45

Part II: Students' responses will vary. Accept responses that are equal to or less than the total budgeted amount shown for each person.

Page 10
1. fries
2. plum
3. live
4. read
5. left
6. thicken
7. agree
8. serpents
9. marching
10. precise
11. hated
12. reclaim
13. admirer
14. slime
15. tidying
16. compliant

Page 14
Students' responses will vary. Accept all reasonable responses.

Page 15
Part I:
2. inconvenient
3. sad
4. big
5. tired
6. thirsty
7. annoying
8. hungry
9. unsightly
10. loud
11. scary
12. large
13. disappointing
14. nerve-racking
15. fun

Part II:
Students' responses will vary. Accept all reasonable responses.

Page 16
Students' responses will vary. Possible responses are listed below.
2. Feelings must be shared at all times.
3. All comfort objects must be taken away from Eights.
4. Females under nine must wear neatly tied hair ribbons at all times.
5. Bragging is not permitted.
6. Teaching younger children is not permitted.
7. Doors must be kept unlocked at all times.
8. Choosing your own mate is not permitted.
9. The committee is permitted to listen in at all times.

Page 20
1. 17 Sickles
2. 16 Sickles and 9 Knuts, or 473 Knuts
3. about 164 scoops
4. 3 Chocolate Frogs
5. 1 Galleon and 12 Sickles
6. 15 Knuts
7. 31 Knuts, or 1 Sickle and 2 Knuts
8. No, because he needs 51 Galleons, which is 800 Sickles and 1,943 Knuts. He has only 800 Sickles and 1,942 Knuts, or 50 Galleons, 16 Sickles, and 28 Knuts.
9. No, because he needs 4 Sickles and 15 Knuts.
10. 14 Sickles and 2 Knuts, or 408 Knuts

Page 21

Answer Keys

Page 25
1. unicorn
2. centaur
3. merman
4. mermaid
5. Minotaur
6. werewolf
7. faun
8. dryad

Page 26
1. disgusting
2. feathers
3. split
4. laugh
5. enormous
6. commotion
7. earsplitting
8. curious
9. shocking
10. evil
11. whiskerless
12. trembling
13. mocking
14. betrayal

TURKISH DELIGHT

Page 30
Students' responses will vary. Possible responses are listed below.
1. can read it.
2. is just jealous that I am smart enough to read a book that he can't.
3. that I am the one who put the Platinum Blonde Hair-Dye Extra Strong in his hair tonic bottle.
4. that I did it with the special power in my eyes.
5. is just mad because I can do math problems in my head and he can't.
6. that I already have a plan to scare Miss Trunchbull and get the house back.
7. that my special power is causing the writing on the chalkboard and not a ghost.
8. that they don't care if I stay with them or Miss Honey.

Page 31
Students' responses will vary. Possible responses are listed below.

Matilda
  Traits: kind, intelligent, brave, loving, has special powers
  Goal: To get Miss Honey's house back for her; to punish people who are mean to kids.
Miss Honey
  Traits: kind, caring, a teacher, loves children, scared of Miss Trunchbull
  Goal: To help Matilda; to get her house back.
Mr. Wormwood
  Traits: not smart, a cheat, car salesman who sells stolen cars, mean, impatient
  Goal: To make lots of money.
Miss Trunchbull
  Traits: mean, hates children, loud, bad temper, likes to hurt children
  Goal: To run a school without children; to keep every one afraid of her.

Page 37
Students' estimates may vary. Accept all reasonable estimates.
1. about $7,200.00
2. about $6,000.00
3. about $6,800.00
4. about $8,000.00
5. about $6,000.00
6. Students' responses will vary. Accept all reasonable responses.

Page 38
1. relieves pain and fever
2. treats burns and frostbite
3. treats malaria
4. treats snakebites
5. treats heart failure
6. treats pneumonia, rheumatic fever, scarlet fever, and other diseases
7. used in antiseptics
8. used in chemotherapy for children's leukemia and to fight Hodgkin's disease
9. treats asthma, hay fever, and low blood pressure
10. treats fevers

Answer Keys

Page 42

Students' reasons for each gift will vary. Accept all reasonable responses.

1. King Azaz: box of words
2. Alec Bings: telescope
3. The Soundkeeper: package of sounds
4. The Mathemagician: magic staff

5–8. Students' responses will vary. Accept all reasonable responses.

Page 43

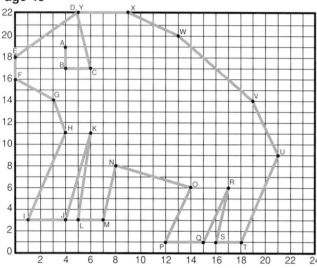

Who helped Milo the most? ___Tock___

Page 47

1. weather va<u>ne</u>
2. <u>qua</u>rry
3. <u>t</u>rap door
4. <u>s</u>quire
5. vi<u>p</u>er
6. <u>m</u>anuscript
7. <u>s</u>parrow
8. scabbar<u>d</u>
9. tapestry
10. <u>c</u>orridor
11. <u>e</u>ffigy
12. <u>th</u>reshold

A	S	M	O	D	E	U	S
9	7	6	10	8	11	2	7

P	O	I	S	O	N	T	E	E	T	H	'S
5	10	4	7	10	1	3	11	11	3	12	7

D	E	N
8	11	1

Page 48

Students' responses will vary. Possible responses are listed below.

Matthias is impulsive, kind, brave, courageous, wise, and encouraging, and has a natural ability with weapons.

Cluny the Scourge is big, tough, evil, heartless, cruel, and fearsome.

Matthias and Cluny the Scourge have a sword fight during which Matthias tricks Cluny and wins the conflict. Matthias wins by using logic rather than physical strength.

Page 54

1. African elephant, blue whale
2. lion, giraffe, arctic fox, greater Indian rhinoceros, gorilla, dingo, common hamster
3. blue whale
4. 54 years
5. 28 years
6. Students' responses will vary. One possible response: human, gorilla, giraffe, dingo, fox
7. 90 years, 120 years
8. 40 times
9. Students' responses will vary. Accept all reasonable responses.
10. Students' responses will vary. Accept all reasonable responses.

Page 59

Students' responses will vary. Possible responses are listed below.

1. ghostlike
2. capable of being easily led, taught, or controlled
3. having to do with the physical body
4. not easily described
5. strikingly less important than what came before
6. suffering from trouble with bile or the liver
7. evil
8. having no body, form, or substance
9. fear
10. a raised platform

Page 60

Students' responses will vary. Possible responses are listed below.

Meg's Goal: Meg's goal is to defeat the Dark Thing and save her father and brother.

Meg's Actions: Meg tessers with Mrs. Whatsit, Mrs. Who, and Mrs. Which. She asks Mrs. Whatsit to take her to her father. Meg has the courage to enter the strange town. She tries to protect Charles Wallace from the man in the CENTRAL Central Intelligence Center. She uses Mrs. Who's glasses to reach her father. Meg risks her life to save Charles Wallace from IT.

Mrs. Whatsit leads Meg and the others to the cavern of the Happy Medium.

Mrs. Who gives her glasses to Meg to use at a time when Meg is in peril.

Mrs. Which tells Meg that she has something that IT doesn't have.

Happy Medium shows the children that the Dark Thing can be overcome.

Aunt Beast heals Meg after she is frozen.